A Manager's Guide
To Speaking
And Listening

A Manager's Guide
To Speaking
And Listening

The Integrated Approach

By J. Campbell Connelly

AMERICAN MANAGEMENT ASSOCIATION, INC.
NEW YORK

Foreword

This handbook on communication for management and professional staff is divided into three sections. Part I is devoted to *oral* presentation—that is, effective speaking. Part II is devoted to *aural* awareness and improvement—in other words, effective listening. Part III shows how these interrelated aspects of communication are used in a recurring and highly important situation: the problem-solving conference. This is the first time that the oral and aural facets of communication, both of them critical, have been integrated into a single suggested program for professional and personal development. Yet it is the integration of these two communication processes that has had such an impact on business and industry.

Speech, traditionally, has been treated separately; where taught, it has been offered as a single course. Listening has only recently been considered at all. Now, however, we have Dr. Ralph Nichols, director of rhetoric at the University of Minnesota, to thank for the fact that it too is offered as a single course in a few of our universities.

But speaking and listening are not separate communication activities. The success of the one depends upon the success of the other. To communicate effectively, managers should be exposed to this integrated approach.

Besides, integration goes even further than speaking and listening. If you're going to talk, you certainly want what you say to be both heard and understood. If you're going to listen and observe, you should know not only how to do both but also how to remember what you hear and see and be able to recall it usefully. For this reason the memory element of communication (input–storage–search–recall) must be taken into account. No matter how effectively you can now recall what you hear, you should do much better after studying this handbook.

The integrated program outlined here will consist, then, of speaking, listening and observing, and remembering. By practicing the recommended methods and techniques, you should be able to put a keener edge on your managerial communication skills and carry out your responsibilities more efficiently and successfully.

This is a *small* book, designed for busy management people. All unnecessary material has been deleted; only practical information is included. Consequently, the book can be used as a ready reference and also as an outline for management classes in oral and aural communication.

Your future success may depend on the degree to which you can develop your communication abilities.

J. C. C.

Acknowledgments

My sincerest gratitude to:

- Douglas Chaffee and Karl Orimenko for their permission to use the drawings in this book. These drawings were originally created for use in my classes and lent themselves admirably to the book.
- Duane Kent for developing the management and non-management percentile norms which were so essential for the retention measurements.
- My wife, Beverly, for her typing, retyping, editing, and proofing of the manuscript.
- My daughter, Charlene, who unselfishly sacrificed our time together, not only for the writing of this book but also for the hundreds of evening teaching and survey hours which made the book possible.
- The thousands of students without whom this book would never have been written.

Contents

Introduction

To communicate is to convey information from one person to another person or persons or from one group to another group. On the surface this sounds like a comparatively simple procedure. There are, however, six factors which must be taken into consideration:

1. Reception.
2. Sensation.
3. Perception.
4. Evaluation.
5. Decision.
6. Action.

Any of these six factors can mean the difference between successful or unsuccessful communication. You must be, not only constantly, but also consciously aware of them to be a successful communicator—and in your position you can't afford to be anything else.

First, you must be unequivocally certain that your complete message is being received and that it is affecting the recipient. This takes care of one factor: *reception*. The remaining five will determine both the clarity of your relayed message and the accuracy with which the final recipient receives it. Over these factors in communication you have no control once your message is on its way.

These five factors depend solely on the recipient. They depend on how much of your message he recalls and on his *perception* and the degree to which it has been developed. They depend upon his *evaluation* not only of what you told him but of how you told it to him.

Together, perception and evaluation determine the *decision* the recipient will make. The *action* taken will be a result of the total communication process. It will depend to a great extent on your—the sender's—frame of reference, as well as the receiver's, at that particular time.

Your background and your knowledge of the recipient's background both are crucial to the receipt of your message. Cultural development, education, religion, mores, morals, and prejudices all have their impact on·the six factors in communication. This is why it is so important for you to know the receiver's strengths and weaknesses and his reaction to words which affect him emotionally.

You should make certain, even where words are identical, that the two of you are thinking about the same thing. Many times communication has failed because of semantic misunderstandings which both the sender and the receiver were totally unaware of. Words have different meanings for the same people at different times and places, especially when these words affect the emotions. If the receiver does not like a word that you, as the sender, are giving him, he may subconsciously change it, and this word change will affect the meaning of your message.

Moreover, your message may be passed from person to person. In this case word changes are almost bound to take place—in fact, many times it is difficult to reconcile the final version of the message with the original. Then there are situations where the words are not changed but a different vocal emphasis is given to them. This changed emphasis, too, can affect the emotions, either negatively or positively.

Immediate feedback is important to be sure that your recipient has received the message as you gave it. This feedback may not be necessary at all times, especially if you generally relay messages to the same people. But you will do well to use the feedback system until you are absolutely certain that you and the recipient are sharing the same words, meanings, and understanding; that you are in empathy with each other and are communicating effectively.

Good communication reduces frustration on the job. It takes less time, and is less costly, than poor communication. Obviously, training in effective speaking and writing should be incorporated into every management development program. But anyone in management who thinks his communication skills are adequate just because he's completed courses in public speaking and report writing is jeopardizing his future success. He needs both oral and aural training.

Most management personnel spend between 80 and 90 percent of their time in listening. Most of their decisions are based on what they hear and how they hear it. So, until you know the listening habits of your recipient or audience and are able to deal with them satisfactorily, you will continue to have communication difficulties and frustrations.

In this age of expanding technology, of exploding knowledge and sophisticated communication devices, the weakest element in communication is the human element. It is the goal of the integrated approach to minimize this element of human weakness and so reduce the waste time and expense of communication in business and industry, in education, and in government.

I. ORAL COMMUNICATION
Speech Improvement

*Poise: Some Pointers on Deportment,
The Right Stance, Don't Give Yourself
Away. New Habits: How to Breathe
Correctly, Avoiding Lazy Lips, To
Lower Pitch of Voice, Keep Your
Uvula Limber, Control of the Tongue,
Eye Contact, Vocal Projection,
Beautiful Nasal Tones. Speed. Don't Be
Discouraged.*

The drawings in Part I are the work of Karl Orimenko.

A professional approach to speech improvement will
1. Make you a sought-after speaker.
2. Teach you to enjoy speaking before others.
3. Enable you to make your presentations creative.
4. Improve your poise and self-confidence.
5. Give you new stature with your colleagues.
6. Help you to make a good impression for your company.
7. Make you conscious of yourself but not self-conscious.

Developing your speech potential to a high level will not guarantee you automatic advancement. You must have the flair, the imagination expected of a manager, be capable of generating the ideas and making the decisions on which the future of any organization depends. But with the ability to communicate your ideas clearly, confidently, creatively, interestingly, and persuasively you will have every advantage over your tongue-tied colleagues.

Some of the most highly experienced executives and brilliant professional workers in your company are probably very interested in stereo and hifi. They will buy nothing but the finest matched components for their consoles. They spend hundreds and thousands of dollars to get the "just right" combination which will achieve the exact tonal qualities they demand. Yet these uniquely trained and motivated people seem to ignore the best built-in "hifi set" in the world: the human voice.

Since the training of that human voice to near-perfection costs far less than a hifi console, and since this training may enable you to achieve greater status in your chosen profession and company, why not make it a part of your personal development program?

An oral presentation can be either dry or dramatically dynamic. This depends, largely, on how much formal speech training the person making it has had. You may have a natural aptitude for speaking before groups, or you may be timid in such situations. In either case, you can be a more effective speaker—with training.

Pick up several good books on effective speaking and they will give you certain keys to self-improvement. They will suggest that you develop a keen mental attitude, know and understand your audience, develop a speech outline, make your information clear and interesting, and enunciate your words clearly. They will urge you to be persuasive, forceful, and direct. Generally they add that if only you will remember to "be yourself," your problems will be over. The trouble is that most books neglect to tell you specifically how to do all this. It is, therefore, the ever important *how* that will concern us here.

Remember, how much you improve will depend on how much effort you put forth, how much time you have available, and how interested and motivated you are. No one can do the job for you. It's practice that will make you perfect— if you practice perfectly.

POISE

YOU MAY BELIEVE that a speaker's first problem is "over-nervousness." We use this phrase to distinguish the state of mind it suggests from the "natural nervousness" which should result from your desire to make your presentation an effective one. You should be overly nervous only when you have not developed your subject matter as fully as you should, you do not know your audience, or you feel vocally untrained.

We shall assume that you have your subject matter well in hand and know something about the audience you are addressing. Therefore, the actual presentation will be your major problem. The professional approach will help you to overcome this problem, and one mark of the professional speaker, of course, is his poise and ease of manner.

Some Pointers on Deportment

It's certainly a fact that the first thing an audience notices about a speaker is his deportment. Impressions are formed—either consciously or subconsciously—while he merely sits, waiting to be introduced. If you seem uncomfortable and disorganized, the audience suspects that your presentation will be pretty much the same. Conversely, if you look confident, well poised, and alert, you will project this feeling to the audience.

Don't adjust your clothing after you have made your appearance. You should have checked yourself beforehand, in front of a mirror. Sit, rather, in a relaxed, comfortable position, your legs crossed at the knee or at the ankle. (The latter position is the only acceptable one for women.) Then, when you've been introduced, don't slouch or lumber from your chair, fumbling for your notes and straightening your tie. Always use your leg muscles when rising from a chair.

Many speakers have no idea how to stand before an audience; they become self-conscious and nervous in the absence of a lectern. However, because you can be a far more effective speaker without a lectern, you should be capable of speaking to an audience without hiding behind one. The lectern too often becomes a crutch. Without it you have more physical freedom and flexibility. You can capture and hold the attention of your audience by the confidence with which you move about on the stage.

A lectern may be supplied for a formal presentation. If you're given one, put it to its original intended use—to hold your notes. Don't lean on it unless you are striving for a definite effect. With practice, you will discover that this technique will gain you a greater command of your listening audience.

Speakers often put their hands in their pockets or fold them in back or in front of the body. These positions, too, are crutches; they take away the poise and dignity of the speaker. Simply stand on the stage with your hands by your side and talk. The only time your hands should move is when you are consciously gesturing. You can put the energy you save by avoiding nervous movements into effective vocal emphasis.

The first thing an audience notices . . .

THE RIGHT STANCE

The following position will be uncomfortable for you for quite some time, but only because it is foreign to you. After you've integrated it into your personality, though, you'll wonder why you didn't always stand this way.

1. Place your feet approximately shoulder-width apart with your weight on the balls of the feet. Let the front portion of each heel (just before it turns into sole) touch the floor.
2. Bend your knees slightly. This takes away strain and helps prevent the knees from shaking. It also gives a more relaxed appearance.
3. Pull your stomach in and up.
4. Pull or tuck your derrière in.
5. Keep your shoulders down and loose.
6. Keep your arms loose.
7. Keep your hands down by your side. Forget them—

. . . is your deportment

don't put them in your pockets or cross them in back
or in front of you.

Be alert to any subconscious hand, body, or head movements. If necessary, have one of your colleagues bring them
to your attention. Only when you become consciously aware
of these unintentional movements can you begin to correct
them.

Acquire the habit of standing comfortably in this manner
whenever you make an oral presentation, looking your audience directly in the eyes. This is an interesting exercise all
by itself. You wonder what the audience is thinking about
you, and they wonder what you are thinking about them.

In fact, you can practice standing like this many times
every day whether during formal business conferences or in
informal conversation. At first you will feel stiff and uncomfortable. Then you will begin to develop much more poise
and self-assurance. You will begin to radiate this new confidence in your own abilities. Soon you will feel uncomfortable if you revert to your old habits of standing.

Don't Give Yourself Away

What about grammatical errors and slips of the tongue?
Need they betray lack of poise? Not necessarily, although
many speakers give themselves away when they make mis-
takes or when they cannot instantly recall their next thought
phrase.

Actually, minor verbal and grammatical errors may go un-
corrected. In all probability you will be saying the same
words again, and you can then correct them. More serious
is the error of letting the audience become aware that you
have forgotten what you were going to say next. Some
people stutter and stammer in such a predicament; others
make all sorts of grimaces and gestures. However, if you

just stand on the stage and look at your audience intelligently (not blankly or helplessly), no one will ever know what's going on in your mind. You may even move about the stage in a pensive mood. By the time you have done this once or twice, either your thought phrase will have come back or you will be able to improvise. If you stay poised, that is. If you allow yourself to panic, then the only thing that can happen is that your panic will grow.

NEW HABITS

POISE, in short, is one significant aspect of effective speaking that affects your ability to deliver a creative presentation. But it is not the only one. Just as important are breathing and the use of the lips, the tongue, and the various other organs of speech. Much of what you say may be new to you, and you are going to have to practice the recommended exercises conscientiously. Give yourself plenty of time—you can't expect significant results overnight.

One day an R&D manager asked a speech instructor for help with a presentation. "Very well," said the instructor, "When would you like to begin?" The reply nearly left him speechless. The manager had to present his paper the next day—all he wanted was some pointers. The instructor offered to listen to a "dry run" and was again staggered by the response he got. "Oh, I've already had my dry run. It's just that someone suggested you might give me a few ideas for highlighting the talk."

"How long did you study for your professional degree?" asked the instructor. The R&D man looked at him quizzically but answered, "Nine years." The teacher then pointed out gently that no one could expect to improve either his speech or his presentation in a few short hours. It would be grossly unfair and unkind to hear him and evaluate him without having enough time to do any constructive work with him. To do so would only confuse him; later, while he was making the actual presentation, he would be thinking about what the instructor had said instead of concentrating on his subject and evaluating his audience. In fact, preparation for an effective oral presentation should begin one or two years before a person is to represent his company as a speaker.

The manager was smart; he was not an R&D man for nothing. Upon returning from the conference at which he'd spoken, he asked when the next class in basic speech would begin. He not only took the elementary course but went on to the intermediate and advanced classes. Now he knows what the instructor was talking about when he said that it is impossible to improve your speech in a few short hours; that, first, you must break old habits and rid yourself of unnecessary inhibitions. Only then can you really begin to improve.

In other words, it takes just as much training to be able to speak on a professional level as it does to become professionally proficient in any other endeavor. And it is imperative that you continue studying in order to remain at the peak of efficiency.

The suggested exercises are beneficial not only when performed in class. You can also do them at home with the whole family, on your way to and from work, or even at parties. You should *enjoy* doing them.

How to Breathe Correctly

You cannot speak correctly unless you breathe correctly. Diaphragmatic breathing is the key to a pleasant and a well-projected voice. Without diaphragmatic breathing, it is impossible to color your voice or to utilize its full range.

Get the air where it belongs

Think of the air going to the bottom of your stomach. Take a deep breath when you inhale—from the bottom up, not from the top down. Incorrect breathing is the origin of most speakers' troubles. Some schools of speech call this "stomach" breathing. The important thing is to get the air where it belongs: in the *bottom* of the lungs first, not the top. Don't let your shoulders or chest rise when you're taking a breath.

Exercise: The following steps will help you to breathe properly:
1. Put your hand on your stomach.
2. Breathe deeply. Your stomach and your hand should move forward.
3. Now exhale by pulling your diaphragm in. The diaphragm pushes against the lungs and forces the air out.

Don't think of the biological make-up of the voice, the throat, or the palates. Just imagine the air coming through a tube from the lungs and out your mouth.

Repeat this exercise several times a day.

Avoiding Lazy Lips

One reason for your difficulty with some words is that your lips and facial muscles are tight. If you are to be an effective speaker, your lips, facial muscles, and articulating organs must all be flexible.

Lazy lips are one of a speaker's worst enemies. If your lips don't do their share of the work, your speech will be mumbled. The sounds *p, b, m, f,* and *v* will be nearly indistinguishable. Moreover, lazy lips cause a great deal of difficulty with all the vowels. Good vowel formation demands vigorous and well-formed lips.

Exercise: Try this for a practical demonstration:
 1. Think of the words *shirt-sheet-shoot* but don't say them aloud.
 2. Form the lips as though you were going to say the word *sheet.* (Smile, with your lips apart.) Make the *sh* sound that you make when you say the word *sheet.*
 3. Now think of the word *shirt* and form your lips as though you were going to say *shhhh*—the way you would if you were in a room where a baby was sleeping and someone came in. Just make the *sh* sound; don't say the word.
 4. Think of the word *shoot.* First, form your smiling lips as you did for the word *sheet*—make the *sh* sound. While you're still making it, think of the word *shoot* and form your lips to make the new *sh* sound. This is a glide *shooo* sound.

Look in a mirror when doing this important exercise. This will give you an aural, pictorial, muscular, and practical view of it. In fact, do all these exercises in front of a mirror until you know you are doing them correctly.

Exercise: The following exercise is to aid you in strengthening the upper lip muscle. This is the one muscle which gives the greatest amount of trouble.

1. With your lips apart, form a huge smile. Make it just as wide as you can from ear to ear.
2. Now, quickly, shape your lips as though you were going to whistle. (Only, don't.)

After doing this exercise several times, you will notice your facial and lip muscles tiring. To relax, flutter your lips like a horse.

For further practice, now that you have acquired some agility with your lips, try saying all the vowels with your tongue just touching the back of your lower front teeth. Or close your mouth and move your lower jaw from side to side—and repeat with your mouth open. Or make all the foolish-looking faces you can by stretching your mouth and face in all directions. Or flutter your tongue like a Scotchman rolling his *r*'s. At all times be consciously aware of keeping your teeth apart while you talk.

These particular exercises are highly interesting when introduced at parties. You might call them "facial fractures."

Highly interesting when introduced at parties

Put the emphasis on the lower tones

To Lower Pitch of Voice

In these busy days most of us speak in our middle or higher register. For greater effectiveness you should endeavor to lower the pitch of your voice by three full tones. You can learn how just as the baseball rookie learns to control his pitch.

Exercise: A good way to accomplish this is to go up and down the scale vocally with emphasis on the lower tones. Be sure to open your mouth wide and keep your tongue down behind, just touching your lower front teeth.

When doing this scale exercise, voice the word *ah* instead of *do, re, mi,* and so on. Place the *ah* well forward in the mouth and project it to the front, or back, of the room.

This exercise is more effective when done with a piano because it takes more conscious effort to project over the sound of the instrument. However, if you don't have a piano, don't let that prevent you from practicing. You may even end up buying one!

Provided you practice faithfully, you should overcome the normal tendency to speak in a monotone. You should also be able to color your voice and achieve a greater command of your audience by intentionally changing the pitch, volume, and tone of your voice. Remember, put the emphasis on the lower tones and consciously speak in lower tones throughout the day—and night.

KEEP YOUR UVULA LIMBER

The uvula can and does give trouble to a great many speakers. This organ is located at the extreme end of the soft palate. The palate is normally closed, which is one reason why some people speak with a harsh nasal voice. A lazy uvula can make an otherwise potentially beautiful voice sound absolutely ugly.

Exercise: Here are four steps that help to keep your uvula limber:

Say ahhh!

1. Open your mouth wide.
2. Say *ahhh, ahhh.* This will put your uvula in an open position so the sound can be emitted with minimum interference from the uvula.
3. Say *ahhh, ahhh* once again. Now bring the sound up into the nasal regions. This makes for a forced nasal tone.
4. Alternate the forced nasal tone and the open tone. You should be able to feel the uvula open and close.

This exercise should be done several times a day in order to keep your uvula flexible. It is designed specifically for those who speak with a nasal tone. Remember, the uvula must be open for a good, clear tone.

CONTROL OF THE TONGUE

Many potentially fine speakers are ineffective simply because they are not consciously aware of the position of their tongue when they're talking. Their projection is good; they can be heard in the back of the room. But they cannot be understood.

One major reason for their not being understood is that they are swallowing their words. They have no control over their tongue. It is floundering, uncontrolled, all around the mouth. This is what gives their speech a muffled, indistinct sound. The correct placement of the tongue is of the utmost importance for clear, well-projected, unmuffled speech.

. . . Behind, and just touching, your lower front teeth

Exercise: Your tongue may be your worst enemy.

To make sure that you keep from swallowing your words, place your tongue behind, and just touching, your lower front teeth when saying any vowel.

Say the vowels several times daily, using all their various sounds: long, short, and all the others. As you practice, be consciously aware of the various positions of the tongue, and the various pressures of your teeth, on your tongue.

EYE CONTACT

Some schools of speech suggest that you look over the heads of your audience to conquer stage fright or nervousness. This is like talking to a blank wall. The danger is that your speech may go where you are looking—over people's heads.

The only way you can judge the response of the people in your audience is to look them in the eye. There is no substitute for eye-to-eye contact; it is one of the most important

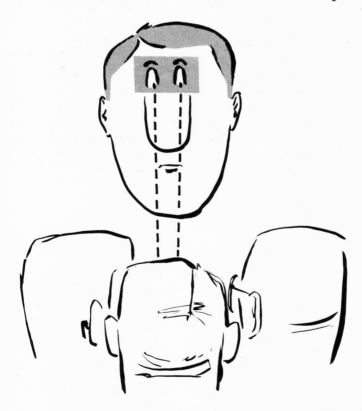

Seeing eye to eye with your colleagues

factors in determining whether your presentation will be truly creative and successful. You can have no conception of how your message is being received unless you can see what reaction your words are inspiring. Only by direct eye contact with your audience can you intelligently vary your presentation.

This is one great advantage that a speaker has over an actor, who has to develop sufficient intuitiveness to be able to *feel* the reaction of his audience. A speaker, with training, can both see the audience and sense this electrical flow from his hearers. True, when the speaker is making a presentation with slides or motion pictures in a dark room, he has only his feeling about the audience to rely on. For this reason you should train yourself, not only to be conscious of the visual reactions of your audience, but to develop a keen sensitivity to their intangible reactions.

Exercise: In small groups, practice looking directly into each individual's eyes. Get accustomed to really seeing eye to eye with your colleagues and associates. Try to get their response to what you're saying. This can sometimes make the difference between a successful and an unsuccessful presentation. It also aids in eliminating some of your unneeded inhibitions.

VOCAL PROJECTION

Now, with the previous exercises behind you, you're ready to develop your vocal projection—like a football player striving for an "educated" toe. The correct use of your speech organs will insure that you're understood, but you must take care to project those well-articulated words to the back of the room. Some people try to do this by shouting. These people can be heard but not understood; you want to be heard and understood.

Exercise: Take a deep diaphragmatic breath (see page 25). When you exhale, say *one* and think of your voice leaving your mouth and actually hitting the back of the room. Repeat this exercise, taking a new diaphragmatic breath for each count. Use all your air on each of these counts. Do this several times daily.

Shouting is uncontrolled speech; projection is controlled speech. For a more sophisticated controlled projection, stand close to a wall and say *one* as though you were talking to someone very near. Then take one step backward and repeat the process. Each time you step back, your projection should be correspondingly greater.

The main difficulty here is that of controlling the pitch of your voice as you increase the distance between you and the wall. Don't let it rise. This exercise takes a great deal of practice; conscious awareness and frequent repetition are necessary.

BEAUTIFUL NASAL TONES

We have said that a pleasant voice can be ruined by a forced nasal quality. Actually, a nasal tone can be one of the

. . . Like a football player with an "educated" toe

ugliest or one of the most beautiful in the English language.

Exercise: Perform the following steps to form the nasal *M* sound correctly:

Feel those vibrations

1. Touch your lips together lightly.
2. Put your tongue behind and just touching your lower front teeth.
3. Hum in your medium range.

Next try the same thing with *N*. This sound is formed in the same manner as *M* except for the position of the tongue. The tip of the tongue is placed on the front of the hard palate just above and behind the upper teeth.

Think of your voice as being out in front of your mouth. Project the humming sound as far as possible. You should feel vibrations on your lips and around your nose; in fact, you will feel these vibrations extending to your throat and chest as you become more proficient in this exercise.

After you do this exercise well, go to the words in the articulation exercises on pages 36–47. Hang on to the *m* and *n* in all of them before saying the vowel or the rest of the word. Some people have difficulty saying the *m* or *n* at the beginning of a word; others, in the middle of a word; and still others, at the end of a word.

SPEED

You can perform all these exercises to perfection while speaking before a group and still not achieve an effective presentation because you spoke too rapidly. This lack of success is usually caused by nervousness or a desire to fiinish the presentation as quickly as possible. You should watch yourself here, or in all probability your speech will be finished too soon—before it starts, in fact.

One of the most practical methods of slowing your speech is to say the following articulation exercises very slowly. Such combinations of words make for extremely useful practice. You must, for example, emphasize your *M* in order for everyone in your audience to differentiate between it and *B*. Exaggeration is the key.

If you are truly aware of your diaphragmatic breathing, lips, facial muscles, tongue, uvula, voice pitch, projection, and nasal tones, you will do these exercises slowly. It is only by doing them both slowly and correctly that you will be able to integrate the benefits into your own improved speech pattern.

SLOW
DOWN
SPEECH

Your speech will be finished before it starts

Exercise: The M Sound

Nonsense Syllables

(m-m-i) (m-i) (mi) (i-m-m) (i-m) (im) (i-m-m-i) (i-m-i) (imi)
(m-m-e) (m-e) (me) (e-m-m) (e-m) (em) (e-m-m-e) (e-m-e) (eme)
(m-m-a) (m-a) (ma) (a-m-m) (a-m) (am) (a-m-m-a) (a-m-a) (ama)
(m-m-o) (m-o) (mo) (o-m-m) (o-m) (om) (o-m-m-o) (o-m-o) (omo)
(m-m-u) (m-u) (mu) (u-m-m) (u-m) (um) (u-m-m-u) (u-m-u) (umu)

Words

made	map	came	am	beaming	anthem
make	match	come	climb	bombing	atom
man	mean	farm	dim	famous	balsam
may	meet	hime	dime	foamy	bedlam
me	mesh	home	dome	hammer	emblem
men	might	name	from	lemon	heroism
mine	mob	same	gem	memory	phantom
much	mood	some	gum	pommel	problem
must	moss	them	lame	rumor	random
my	mouse	time	seem	timber	symptom

B and M

bean-mean	batch-match	bob-bomb	sob-psalm
bit-mitt	bill-mill	rob-rum	lobe-loam
bake-make	beet-meet	mob-mom	robe-roam
boss-moss	bug-mug	hub-hum	rib-rim

Sentences

1. The man's face wore an impenetrable mask.
2. The mummers came to Mary's home on Christmas Eve.
3. Robin Hood's messenger met the Merry Men under the massive elm.
4. The bumblebees and humming birds were murmuring melodiously.
5. You must memorize this poem in twenty minutes.
6. Marion sat meditating by the Mediterranean.
7. Tom grumbled because he had to come home when he wanted to see the new film at the movies.
8. My mother made a warm muff for Mary out of my mink coat.
9. The menacing marsh was the murmurous haunt of flies on summer eves.
10. Moses was known as the meekest man.

Exercise: The N Sound

Nonsense Syllables

(n-n-i)	(n-i)	(ni)	(i-n-n)	(i-n)	(in)	(i-n-n-i)	(i-n-i)	(ini)
(n-n-e)	(n-e)	(ne)	(e-n-n)	(e-n)	(en)	(e-n-n-e)	(e-n-e)	(ene)
(n-n-a)	(n-a)	(na)	(a-n-n)	(a-n)	(an)	(a-n-n-a)	(a-n-a)	(ana)
(n-n-o)	(n-o)	(no)	(o-n-n)	(o-n)	(on)	(o-n-n-o)	(o-n-o)	(ono)
(n-n-u)	(n-u)	(nu)	(u-n-n)	(u-n)	(un)	(u-n-n-u)	(u-n-u)	(unu)

Words

knee	know	seen	lone	bonny	nonage
knit	nine	in	gone	contemplate	pony
not	name	then	lawn	dinner	rainy
gnat	noun	cairn	rain	funny	shiny
nurse	noise	an	vine	gunning	sunny
nut	near	can't	own	honey	tiny
noon	Noah	earn	town	incongruous	tonnage
known	newer	sun	coin	linen	vanish
gnaw	nude	moon	tune	money	whinny

Sentences

1. Anita knits industriously morning, noon, and night.
2. Nan can't earn enough money to buy all the new novels.
3. Nora lives at the corner of Ninetieth Street and Ninth Avenue.
4. Nonresident students often travel late at night and early in the morning.
5. Vachel Lindsay wrote a poem called "The Congo."
6. The knights were confident of victory in the impending conflict.

Exercise: The Two Ng's

Nonsense Syllables

(i-ng-ng)	(i-ng)	(ing)	(i-ng-ng-i)	(i-ng-i)	(ingi)
(e-ng-ng)	(e-ng)	(eng)	(e-ng-ng-e)	(e-ng-e)	(enge)
(a-ng-ng)	(a-ng)	(ang)	(a-ng-ng-a)	(a-ng-a)	(anga)
(o-ng-ng)	(o-ng)	(ong)	(o-ng-ng-o)	(o-ng-o)	(ongo)
(u-ng-ng)	(u-ng)	(ung)	(u-ng-ng-u)	(u-ng-u)	(ungu)

Words

Ng as in song:		Ng as in finger:	
bring	young	anger	languid
clang	hanger	anguish	linger
drink	singer	bangle	longer
fang	wringer	bungle	longest
gong	banging	dinghy	mangle
hung	clinging	diphthongal	mingle
link	doing	England	single
mink	finding	English	stronger
rung	hanging	finger	strongest
song	longing	hanger	wrangle
tang	ringing	hunger	younger
wing	singing	language	youngest

Sentences

1. Mary was nursing a sore finger.
2. The girls were going out on Long Island for the holiday.
3. A gang of younger boys broke up the meeting.
4. Fishing and hunting and trespassing are forbidden in these grounds.
5. Jim is doing a fine piece of work as managing editor of the Newport *Gong.*
6. Learning the English language is a long, hard process for those speaking a foreign tongue.
7. In the olden days in England, the barking of the dogs indicated that the beggars were descending upon the town in great numbers.

Exercise: The P Sound

Nonsense Syllables

(p-p-i) (p-i) (pi) (i-p-p) (i-p) (ip) (i-p-p-i) (i-p-i) (ipi)
(p-p-e) (p-e) (pe) (e-p-p) (e-p) (ep) (e-p-p-e) (e-p-e) (epe)
(p-p-a) (p-a) (pa) (a-p-p) (a-p) (ap) (a-p-p-a) (a-p-a) (apa)
(p-p-o) (p-o) (po) (o-p-p) (o-p) (op) (o-p-p-o) (o-p-o) (opo)
(p-p-u) (p-u) (pu) (u-p-p) (u-p) (up) (u-p-p-u) (u-p-u) (upu)

Words

paper	pack	chop	cap	apple	keeper
party	pad	clap	cape	apron	oppose
people	palm	help	deep	carpet	pepper

pet	peak	hop	ripe	happy	rapid
picture	pin	jump	rope	open	report
pig	pine	keep	ship	paper	separate
place	pole	sleep	shop	people	stupid
pony	pool	steep	slap	stopped	superior
pull	pot	stop	stoop	surprise	suppose
put	puff	up	wipe	upon	typical

B Distinguished from P

rabid-rapid	robing-roping
nabbing-napping	cabby-Cappy
tabbing-tapping	lobbing-lopping
ribbing-ripping	mobbing-mopping

Sentences

1. Do you suppose that Paul appreciates painting and sculpture?
2. Plan a speech improvement program and keep practicing.
3. The pig stopped in surprise and pounced on the table.
4. After the party there was paper all over the carpet.
5. Some spellings represent speech very poorly.

Exercise: The B *Sound*

Nonsense Syllables

(b-b-i)	(b-i)	(bi)	(i-b-b)	(i-b)	(ib)	(i-b-b-i)	(i-b-i)	(ibi)
(b-b-e)	(b-e)	(be)	(e-b-b)	(e-b)	(eb)	(e-b-b-e)	(e-b-e)	(ebe)
(b-b-a)	(b-a)	(ba)	(a-b-b)	(a-b)	(ab)	(a-b-b-a)	(a-b-a)	(aba)
(b-b-o)	(b-o)	(bo)	(o-b-b)	(o-b)	(ob)	(o-b-b-o)	(o-b-o)	(obo)
(b-b-u)	(b-u)	(bu)	(u-b-b)	(u-b)	(ub)	(u-b-b-u)	(u-b-u)	(ubu)

Words

back	began	crib	bob	about	bribery
ball	big	cub	bribe	above	dubious
barn	bird	grab	cab	anybody	fabulous
basket	black	knob	daub	baby	labial
be	blue	rib	jab	cupboard	liberty
bear	boat	rob	jib	fable	nobility
because	book	sob	job	number	robber
bed	both	tab	robe	rabbit	rubbing
been	box	tub	scrub	ribbon	sober
before	boy	web	tube	table	tubing

P Distinguished from B

peak-beak	rip-rib	path-bath
peat-beat	nip-nib	palm-bomb
peer-beer	gyp-jib	pop-bop
peas-bees	tap-tab	par-bar

Sentences

1. Behind the barn are both blackbirds and bluebirds.
2. Anybody who believes that fable is as gullible as a baby.
3. Bob built the biggest building in Columbus.
4. The bear broke the box after he had grabbed it.
5. Grab that scrubbing brush below the cupboard.

Combinations with B and P

babble	noble	rapping	toper
bauble	ribald	pauper	ripple
bubble	sobbing	supple	sopping
cable	turbulent	capable	turpentine

Sentences

1. The Pied Piper played his pipe and compelled the children to leave their play.
2. Some people prefer pumpkin pie, while others prefer plum pudding.
3. Peter planted peas and beans and barley in the spring.
4. The children were blowing soap bubbles in the billiard room.
5. The children happened to be taking a nap when the bell in the neighboring steeple was rung.
6. The boy grappled with the robber bare-handed and thrashed him with a horsewhip.

Exercise: The T *Sound*

Nonsense Syllables

(t-t-i)	(t-i)	(ti)	(i-t-t)	(i-t)	(it)	(i-t-t-i)	(i-t-i)	(iti)
(t-t-e)	(t-e)	(te)	(e-t-t)	(e-t)	(et)	(e-t-t-e)	(e-t-e)	(ete)
(t-t-a)	(t-a)	(ta)	(a-t-t)	(a-t)	(at)	(a-t-t-a)	(a-t-a)	(ata)
(t-t-o)	(t-o)	(to)	(o-t-t)	(o-t)	(ot)	(o-t-t-o)	(o-t-o)	(oto)
(t-t-u)	(t-u)	(tu)	(u-t-t)	(u-t)	(ut)	(u-t-t-u)	(u-t-u)	(utu)

Words

table	take	about	fast	after	butter
tall	taught	asked	feet	better	detail
take	teeth	at	first	kitten	later
teacher	tight	basket	get	letter	lattice
tell	tip	boat	great	mister	metal
ten	ton	but	just	party	motto
time	tool	cat	last	pretty	pitied
to	town	count	left	sister	pouting
today	train	cut	light	wanted	rotate
took	tree	cat	liked	water	totem

D Distinguished from T

deem-team	bad-bat	medal-metal
dean-teen	cad-cat	riding-writing
dear-tear	gad-gat	pedal-petal
din-tin	mad-mat	biding-biting
dame-tame	node-note	herding-hurting
dale-tale	showed-shoat	wading-waiting
dare-tare	booed-boot	madder-matter
dime-time	cooed-coot	kiddy-kitty

With T and D

slept	wiped	tracked	raked	sliced
crypt	draped	hooked	tacked	haste
slipped	looped	locked	past	boost
slapped	erupt	peeked	crossed	best
flopped	backed	talked	just	fist
doped	tucked	jerked	moist	feast

Sentences

1. The teacher taught him to touch his teeth with the tip of his tongue.
2. Betty's little sister wanted to go to the party.
3. Students sometimes use the term "accent" to refer to a dialect.
4. It is better to talk too little than to talk too much.
5. A child with a cleft palate tends to omit certain consonants.

More Combinations with *T* and *D*

bidden	sudden	bounding	satin	bottle
bedding	boding	siding	certain	carting
saddle	coddle	bitten	button	bounty
burden	carding	better	boating	citing

Sentences

1. The bad boy hadn't any excuse for doing such an unkind deed.
2. The driver shouldn't have turned the corner against a red light.
3. The master of the riding school was writing to a friend in Littleton.
4. The broken bottle punctured the tires of the little car and caused an accident.
5. Uncle Don's story of the battle seemed endless to Betty, but completely satisfactory to Teddy.
6. Tom evidently intended to go on a long trip, because he carried a lot of luggage.
7. The clever partners confidently expected to win the game of contract bridge.

Exercise: The D *Sound*

Nonsense Syllables

(d-d-i)	(d-i)	(di)	(i-d-d)	(i-d)	(id)	(i-d-d-i)	(i-d-i)	(idi)
(d-d-e)	(d-e)	(de)	(e-d-d)	(e-d)	(ed)	(e-d-d-e)	(e-d-e)	(ede)
(d-d-a)	(d-a)	(da)	(a-d-d)	(a-d)	(ad)	(a-d-d-a)	(a-d-a)	(ada)
(d-d-o)	(d-o)	(do)	(o-d-d)	(o-d)	(od)	(o-d-d-o)	(o-d-o)	(odo)
(d-d-u)	(d-u)	(du)	(u-d-d)	(u-d)	(ud)	(u-d-d-u)	(u-d-u)	(udu)

Words

day	dab	and	heard	body	audible
dear	dawn	bed	hide	building	edible
did	daze	bread	kind	candy	louder
do	death	could	land	children	medial
dog	deem	did	made	garden	modify
doll	deep	find	need	hidden	muddier
door	dig	good	old	ready	radical
down	dine	had	read	today	radio
draw	ditch	hand	red	under	shady
dress	doom	head	ride	window	sudden

T Distinguished from D

team-deem	bat-bad	note-node
teen-dean	cat-cad	shoat-showed
tear-dear	gat-gad	boot-booed
tin-din	mat-mad	coot-cooed

Combinations with *Other Sounds*

sobbed	cribbed	begged	sagged	moved
robed	jabbed	hugged	fogged	roved
dabbed	lobed	rigged	saved	raved
ribbed	grabbed	tugged	lived	dived
bobbed	bogged	lugged	peeved	believed
bribed	bagged	lagged	loved	shoved

Sentences

1. Dick opened the window and listened to the bird.
2. Reading this drill indifferently will do you no good.
3. It is hidden in the garden under the window.
4. The sound faded until it was just audible.
5. I found some candy in the drawer.

Exercise: The K *Sound*

Nonsense Syllables

(k-k-i)	(k-i)	(ki)	(i-k-k)	(i-k)	(ik)	(i-k-k-i)	(i-k-i)	(iki)
(k-k-e)	(k-e)	(ke)	(e-k-k)	(e-k)	(ek)	(e-k-k-e)	(e-k-e)	(eke)
(k-k-a)	(k-a)	(ka)	(a-k-k)	(a-k)	(ak)	(a-k-k-a)	(a-k-a)	(aka)
(k-k-o)	(k-o)	(ko)	(o-k-k)	(o-k)	(ok)	(o-k-k-o)	(o-k-o)	(oko)
(k-k-u)	(k-u)	(ku)	(u-k-k)	(u-k)	(uk)	(u-k-k-u)	(u-k-u)	(uku)

Words

cake	cool	back	brick	accident	cookery
call	couch	black	cook	basket	decorate
came	cow	book	hawk	because	likeable
can	cried	coke	like	biscuit	likely
car	cut	look	luck	breakfast	local
cat	keep	make	neck	cocoa	occur
catch	keg	milk	seek	making	second
come	kick	take	took	o'clock	walking
could	kind	thank	walk	picnic	wicked
count	think	kitten	work	picture	working

K Distinguished from G

tag-tack	lug-luck	meager-meeker	haggle-hackle
lag-lack	chug-chuck	tagging-tacking	hogging-hawking
rag-rack	brig-brick	bagging-backing	Deagan-deacon
nag-knack	prig-prick	stagger-stacker	sagging-sacking

Sentences

1. Take the carrots and cabbages from the basket.
2. I like to drink cocoa for breakfast.
3. The cock crows at break of day.
4. Carl gave me a picture book for Christmas.
5. An octave is a musical interval of eight diatonic degrees.
6. Correction of defective consonants comes through careful practice.

Exercise: The G *Sound*

Nonsense Syllables

(g-g-i)	(g-i)	(gi)	(i-g-g)	(i-g)	(ig)	(i-g-g-i)	(i-g-i)	(igi)
(g-g-e)	(g-e)	(ge)	(e-g-g)	(e-g)	(eg)	(e-g-g-e)	(e-g-e)	(ege)
(g-g-a)	(g-a)	(ga)	(a-g-g)	(a-g)	(ag)	(a-g-g-a)	(a-g-a)	(aga)
(g-g-o)	(g-o)	(go)	(o-g-g)	(o-g)	(og)	(o-g-g-o)	(o-g-o)	(ogo)
(g-g-u)	(g-u)	(gu)	(u-g-g)	(u-g)	(ug)	(u-g-g-u)	(u-g-u)	(ugu)

Words

girl	geese	dig	log	buggy	legal
garden	gale	beg	bog	again	aghast
gave	game	big	fog	ago	brigade
got	gauze	bug	keg	began	cigar
go	gift	dog	rag	figure	magazine
good	goat	egg	rogue	finger	regard
great	gout	frog	sprig	hungry	stagger
green	gum	leg	stag	organ	trigger
guess	gun	pig	vague	sugar	vigorous

K Distinguished from G

kill-gill	code-goad	tack-tag	luck-lug
cab-gab	coat-goat	lack-lag	chuck-chug
cap-gap	coal-goal	rack-rag	brick-brig
cad-gad	core-gore	knack-nag	prick-prig

Sentences

1. Grace has gone to the garden to get some grapes.
2. The girl gave the hungry pig his dinner.
3. My grandfather has a green buggy.
4. The dog began to growl at the goat.
5. He forgot his hunger and staggered through the fog.

Exercise:

Selections for E Practice

1. After life's fitful fever he sleeps well.—SHAKESPEARE

2. Fair is foul, and foul is fair:
   Hover through the fog and filthy air.—SHAKESPEARE

3. The fair breeze blew, the white foam flew,
   The furrow followed free;
   We were the first that ever burst
   Into that silent sea.—COLERIDGE

4. Swiftly, swiftly, flew the ship,
   Yet she sailed softly too.—COLERIDGE

5. All are at one now, roses and lovers,
   Not known of the cliffs and the fields and the sea.
   Not a breath of the time that has been hovers
   In the air now soft with a summer to be.
   Not a breath shall there sweeten the seasons hereafter
   Of the flowers or the lovers that laugh now or weep
   When as they that are free now of weeping and laughter
   we shall sleep.—SWINBURNE

Exercise:

Selections for W Practice

1. The water, like a witch's oils,
   Burnt green and blue and white.—COLERIDGE

2. Why, let the stricken deer go weep,
   The hart ungalled play;
   For some must watch while some must weep,
   So runs the world away.—SHAKESPEARE

3. Why with the time do I not glance aside
   To new-found methods and to compounds strange?
   Why write I still all one, ever the same,
   And keep invention in a noted weed,
   That every word doth almost tell my name,
   Showing their birth, and where they did proceed?
   O! know, sweet love, I always write of you,
   And you and love are still my argument.—SHAKESPEARE

Exercise:

Sentences for S and Z

1. Breathiness is often associated with excessive softness in speech.

2. Nasality, which has two chief causes, is characterized by nasal resonance in nonnasal sounds.

3. Good speakers and readers inhale during pauses between phrases.

4. The splendor falls on castle walls and snowy summits old in story.—TENNYSON

5. Speak the speech, I pray you, as I pronounced it to you, trippingly on the tongue; but if you mouthe it, as many of your players do, I had as lief the town-crier spoke my lines.
   —SHAKESPEARE

Exercise:

Selections for General Practice

1. Was this the face that launch'd a thousand ships,
   And burnt the topless towers of Ilium?—MARLOWE

2. Softly sweet, in Lydian measures,
   Soon he sooth'd his soul to pleasures.—DRYDEN

3. The clouds were pure and white as flocks new shorn
   And fresh from the clear brook, sweetly they slept
   On the blue fields of heaven, and there crept
   A little noiseless noise among the leaves
   Born of the very sigh that silence leaves,
   For not the faintest motion could be seen
   Of all the shades that slanted o'er the green.—KEATS

4. Sleep is a reconciling,
   A rest that peace begets;
   Shall not the sun rise smiling
   When fair at even it sets?—JOHN DOWLAND

5. There is no frigate like a book
   To take us lands away,
   Nor any coursers like a page
   Of prancing poetry.

   This traverse may the poorest take
   Without oppress of toll;
   How frugal is the chariot
   That bears a human soul!—EMILY DICKINSON

6. A flock of sheep that leisurely pass by,
   One after one; the sound of rain, and bees
   Murmuring; the fall of rivers, winds, and seas,
   Smooth fields, white sheets of water, and pure sky;
   I have thought of all by turns, and yet do lie
   Sleepless! and soon the small birds' melodies
   Must hear, first uttered from my orchard trees;
   And the first cuckoo's melancholy cry.—WORDSWORTH

DON'T BE DISCOURAGED

You shouldn't let yourself become discouraged because of the way you sound while developing your new speech habits. You will, of course, sound horrible—even worse than you look while doing your "facial fracture" exercises!

Remember, you have many old habits to break before you can expect to improve your speech to any noticeable degree. Also, you have many inhibitions which you must eliminate. The exercises in this book should aid you in overcoming both these roadblocks to creative speech. And remember that your success in your career may depend not only on your professional abilities but also on your ability to express your ideas clearly and creatively.

Remember, too, that within a short time your audience

will have retained only a small part of what you have said. Keep this in mind and be determined to increase that percentage by using the methods described here—that is, by making your presentation come alive.

To sum up: The probability of your presentation's being creative and interesting will be greatly increased if you—

1. Hope sincerely to inform and interest your audience.
2. Are consciously aware of yourself but not self-conscious.
3. Can project your personality.
4. Have put to good use the suggestions for speech improvement outlined in these pages.
5. Will take into account the listening weaknesses of your audience.
6. Honestly want to be of service and value to your organization and your audience.

Not only must you motivate yourself, but you must also motivate your audience. Let your personality speak, allowing your listeners to be aware of your interest in your subject. If you can develop vocal individuality, so much the better. Integrate this individuality into your personality; project this trained, accumulated personality to your audience and you'll have that audience with you all the way.

You *are* a professional. Just perfect your techniques of oral communication and you will *sound* like a professional!

II. AURAL COMMUNICATION
Listening, Observing, and Remembering

Your Mental Computer. The One Bad Listening Habit. Empathy in Listening. Listening Peaks. Memory and Its Improvement: The Whole Memory System, The Spaced Memory System, The Basic Laws of Association. More Memory Systems: The Incompleted Method, The Motor Method, The Time Method, The Mental Recap Method, The Conscious Storage Method. Remembering Names and Faces. Miscellaneous Factors in Effective Listening: Efficiency Peaks, Age, Semantics. Analytical Listening. Observation with All the Senses.

The drawings on pages 54–77 and 91–96 are by Karl Orimenko. Those on pages 80–86 are by Douglas Chaffee.

Most managers believe that by mastering the methods and techniques of oral communication they will be 100 percent effective as speakers. This is not necessarily true. Being 100 percent perfect in oral communication is being only 50 percent prepared as a speaker or communicator.

To be 100 percent prepared in communication, you must also be aware of—and trained in—the art of aural communication. You must understand the human processes of listening, observing, and remembering.

In their popular book called *Are You Listening?* [1] Ralph G. Nichols and Leonard A. Stephens declare that an audience with no formal training in listening wll be able to recall, immediately, only about 50 percent of the material presented by a speaker. Two months later, that figure will have dropped to 25 percent.

Retention can, of course, be improved by training. Survey findings in industry [2] show an improvement of approximately 70 to 80 percent in immediate retention and an improvement of approximately 140 percent in retention after two months.

[1] McGraw-Hill Book Company, New York, 1957.
[2] Results of surveys made by the author over a six-year period.

Retention after six months has been about 52 percent; after a full year, about 51 percent—in both cases an improvement of better than 100 percent over the two months' retention before training.

But this sort of training is still, unfortunately, the exception. You have got to assume that most of the time you will be addressing audiences that are "illiterate" so far as listening, observing, and remembering are concerned. In fact, you are just as responsible for knowing and counteracting your audience's poor listening habits as you are for developing your oral communication abilities.

Your greatest challenge as a speaker and communicator is not only to get the audience's attention but to keep it for the duration of your presentation. *Attention is the secret of retention.* If you can capture it and hold it, people will be able to retain and recall a greater percentage of what you tell them.

There are innumerable listening traps lying in wait for people, innumerable ways in which they are prone to dissipate their attention. You must be consciously aware of this likelihood of mental dissipation, and you must devote your energies to preventing your audience or the individual recipient of your message from falling into those lurking traps. That's why it's so important for you to integrate the methods and techniques of communication into your personality to such a degree that they become second nature to you, so that your presentation almost takes care of itself and you can concentrate on observing its effect on your hearers.

Until audiences become trained in the art of listening, in short, the speaker's job is going to be a demanding one. The aural-improvement approach to communication makes it even more difficult but, at the same time, more gratifying because every listener will come away from your presentation with more information.

What more could you possibly desire from an audience?

Your Mental Computer

Your mind operates like a computer. Just as the computer is no good at all if it is not programmed properly, so, too, your mind is inefficient if you neglect its programming.

Indeed, the human mind is the oldest computer in the world. The next oldest, probably, is the abacus. Now, centuries later, comes the complex electronic computer. None of these is more efficient than the person operating it.

A computer has four prime activities: input, storage, search, and recall. The only trouble with your mental computer is that you have not given it sufficient conscious input that it will consciously store and consciously recall the information—correctly—when you consciously search for a piece of stored information.

As you can see, the key word here is *conscious*. The main thing is to make *conscious* inputs to your mind with the *conscious* intention of recalling them at some later time. Also, you can *consciously* tell your mind what you want to store and how long you want to store it for future recall.

Some modern memory systems are based on making ridiculous or fantastic associations. Why bother conjuring these up when the facts and figures that you want to store and recall are quite logical? Logical associations are best utilized in a memory system for logical, intelligent people.

You can improve your memory, in short, without wasting time learning any new tricks or so-called new systems. As a matter of fact, you already have the best possible built-in memory system, whose capabilities are superior to those of any modern-day computer. All you have to do is develop it.

Your only difficulty has been that no one has ever told you how to use your mind properly so as to recall information with ease. You are operating at only about 25 percent efficiency. You can, however, operate at approximately 90 percent efficiency.

THE ONE BAD LISTENING HABIT

The authors of *Are You Listening?* cite six bad listening habits. In all probability, however, there is only one bad listening habit: *mental dissipation*, or *mind wandering*. All the others are contributors to it.

Mental dissipation falls into two categories—conscious and subconscious. It is the subconscious sort that is so costly to management, industry, and the individual, that results in illiterate listening, and that robs us of valuable information. Subconscious mental dissipation must be overcome so that communication will be a more effective management tool.

The only way to overcome this type of mind wandering is through a determined effort and the realization that we do lapse into a subconscious state of listening when attending meetings or even just spending an hour or two with friends. One good technique to keep from succumbing to

There is only one bad listening habit

this kind of lethargy is to make a mental note to yourself—right now—that you will try to pull up short whenever you begin to fall into one of the traps contributing to mental dissipation. Just by using this simple method (which may not be too easy), you will many times find yourself drawing back from a good old-fashioned "brown study."

To communicate effectively, you must know these traps so well that you use them habitually. Only then can you be 100 percent prepared.

We list here nine listening traps or contributors to mental dissipation. Some are conscious, others subconscious.

Contributor No. 1 (conscious): Considering the Subject Uninteresting. An amazing percentage of workers—including both managerial and professional people—decide in advance that a talk or conference is going to be boring. They take the attitude that they couldn't care less. Or, after hearing the speaker's opening words, they become disinterested,

He takes the attitude that he couldn't care less

go off on their own mental tangents, and refuse to listen. How can they evaluate what he's said unless they hear him all the way out?

The speaker must have something to say or management wouldn't have him there. So listen to him! If he has only one idea that you can use sometime in the future, then your time and effort will not have been in vain. If you don't listen, if you persist in your attitude that his subject is uninteresting, you will be the loser. Always take the positive approach in listening and you'll never be wrong.

Contributor No. 2 (subconscious): Evaluating the Speaker Instead of the Speech. It's pretty absurd not to listen to a presentation simply because you don't approve of some part of the speaker's dress or his delivery. These should have no bearing on what the speaker may say, but many otherwise intelligent people seem to feel they do. How often we hear comments like "Oh, I just couldn't listen to him because he

Close your eyes to the lack of style

You let your emotions get away from you

had such a nasal twang." Or "I was put off him right away because of that hideous suit he was wearing."

Agreed that it's sometimes difficult to listen to a speaker because of his manner or appearance. However, we're not there to evaluate either his personality or his sartorial judgment. We are there to hear him through.

If you do consciously catch yourself whenever you rate the speaker instead of the speech, you're on the right road to improvement in this listening area. Close your eyes to the lack of style or the loud jacket. Consciously ignore the rasping voice. Once more, conscious awareness is the key.

Contributor No. 3 (conscious or subconscious): Becoming Emotionally Involved. This is the first of two contributors to bad listening which affect the emotions, so that control is difficult. A speaker may inadvertently, with a phrase or two, show utter disregard for an idea you hold dear or a project on which you may be working. Naturally you become upset.

Instead of thinking constructively about what the speaker is saying, and listening to him until he finishes, you let your emotions get away from you. You begin plotting questions calculated to embarrass him.

Sometimes, during oral presentations, statements are made deliberately to stimulate the audience's emotions, but they often backfire. This technique is not a good one for a speaker to use—it may lose him his audience instead of stimulating it. You, the listener, must keep an open mind. Perhaps, after the speaker has been talking for a while, he will explain himself to your satisfaction, so that you will no longer be tempted to ask those embarrassing questions.

There is no need for him to know that you fell, briefly, into this listening trap of becoming emotionally involved in what he said.

Contributor No. 4 (conscious): Listening Only for Facts. Listening specifically for facts has been a way of life for most of us these many years. Many of us were taught in school to listen this way and have carried the habit over into business and industry. As a result, through no fault of our own, we find it difficult to listen for *ideas*.

Unable to do anything with the information recorded

To quote from W. H. Pyle in *The Psychology of Learning* [3]:

The most important thing about an idea is its meaning. The meaning of an idea is another idea closely associated with it. Since an idea may have many such associations, it may have many meanings. The most important meaning of an idea is the use to which the thing represented by it may be put. Of all the things that the idea of an object may bring to our mind, what most concerns us is what we can do with the thing, how we can make it serve our purposes, how it is likely to affect us, whether it will harm us or do us good.

Few people can spot the main idea in a presentation. Yet knowing the facts without understanding the idea behind them is like having a photographic mind and not being able to do anything with the information recorded.

There are, it's true, presentations which are given simply to dispense facts. Everybody present already understands the idea back of them and is there to get supporting material. In general, however, the first mental task in listening to a presentation is to grasp this main idea. It should come immediately after the speaker's introductory anecdotes and remarks—that is, within the first two or three minutes. In all probability, it will occur again in the middle of the speech and again near the end. It's the old story of "tell 'em what you're gonna tell 'em, tell 'em, and then tell 'em what you told 'em."

The idea may, of course, be couched in different words. In this way the speaker makes certain that all his listeners, whatever their background and level of education, will grasp it.

Next time you attend church, ask someone on the way out what the sermon was about. Ask several people. You will be several times surprised at our human tendency to be just fact listeners, overlooking the idea the facts are designed to support.

[3] Warwick & York, Inc., Baltimore, 1928.

A sure way of not getting what the speaker said

Contributor No. 5 (conscious): Taking Copious Notes. Excessive note taking is one of the surest ways of not getting what the speaker said. It is next to impossible to write down everything he says, yet there are people who try to do just that. They usually wind up with nothing—just a lot of scribbles and scratchings which they are unable to decipher. This is not only a waste of time and money but also a waste of effort. About all it gets you is frustration.

A good speaker should be capable of painting idea pictures with his words. Remember plays in the old days of radio? The actors had to have this picture-painting ability. If they didn't, they soon were out of work. And, TV or no TV, today's speaker is in the same position.

What does painting idea pictures have to do with taking notes? Everything.

There are two types of note-taking systems which demand that a speech be logically organized. The first is *the keyword method*. This is used when the speaker is expounding a rather simple idea, not a compound or complex one. When you get the idea picture, you jot it down with one key word. The speaker should paint his picture so well that you can almost see it. Not everyone in the audience will necessarily use the same key word for the same picture; but they will all, with their different key words, be recording the same idea.

The second method of note taking that requires a well-organized presentation is the *summary method.* Here the ideas can be complex or compound. The speaker must still paint idea pictures with his words, but this time you use a phrase or even a whole sentence to bring back each picture for you. Never more than two phrases or one sentence, though. If you write too long, you may miss the speaker's next thought.

A combination of phrases and key words, or a series of key words, may of course be used. Choose whichever system you prefer, but stick with that one for greatest effectiveness.

Still a third method of taking notes may have to be used when a speech is not well organized or not organized at all. This is the *fact-principle method.* Draw a line down the center of your note pad and, when the speaker mentions a fact, list it. When he mentions a principle, list it. After he's through (and only then), try to connect the facts with the principles. Sometimes you will discover that it's impossible to connect any of them. In this case you will know exactly what the speaker had to say: nothing.

Whatever your method, the time to jot down your notes is when the speaker is making a transition or telling an anecdote. Sometimes he will give you two or three different aspects of the same idea; obviously you need make a note of it only once. Just a little practice will help a great deal.

Contributor No. 6 (conscious or subconscious): Faking Attention—The Wide-Asleep Listener. Literally faking attention is a conscious act. Moreover, it is unforgivably rude. To waste your own and everyone else's time and effort is in itself unthinkable, but to imagine that you are deceiving the speaker is the worst kind of naiveté. Any trained speaker

Are you a "wide-asleep" listener?

can tell by just a quick glance into the eyes of a particular listener whether he is faking. If you don't want to listen to him, you'll do better to stay away in the first place.

However, your mind may automatically go off on a mental tangent in spite of yourself, with no conscious awareness on your part. This is just as disastrous as deliberate faking even though it happens unintentionally. It may, in extreme cases, turn you into a "wide-asleep" listener.

Take the Case of the Wide-Asleep Committee Chairman. One of his members had been addressing the group for only a short time when the chairman was observed just staring straight ahead. The speaker moved to the right and then to the left—and got no reaction. He stopped talking. Nothing. He moved toward the door. Still nothing. Finally he turned the door knob, opened the door, and exited without getting the slightest response from the chairman. So, one by one, each of the committee members stood up and left. When the

The extent of the distracting influence

chairman came to, if he ever did, he must have been extremely embarrassed. Students are notoriously expert at wide-asleep listening, conscious or subconscious. But anyone can qualify.

Contributor No. 7 (conscious): Letting Yourself Be Distracted. How easily are you diverted from what a speaker is saying? Probably it depends on the speaker himself (his ability to hold your interest), the extent of the distracting influence, and your current state of mind. These factors also will determine the remedy.

A meeting can be demoralized by a series of small distractions. The next time you attend one, just notice what happens if someone arrives late. Notice what happens if someone drops something or is overcome by a series of sneezes. Notice what happens if someone is called out of the session. Yes, you guessed it. All eyes go toward that person and the speaker is left standing. Should someone drop a few coins on the floor, the speaker might just as well have saved his breath.

A skillful speaker or chairman can regain his audience's attention—and his train of thought—with a minimum of fuss. You, the listener, can cooperate by disciplining yourself to resist distractions.

Contributor No. 8 (conscious or subconscious): Avoiding Difficult Listening. Most of us fall into this trap because we have had no formal listening training. Just as some people never learn how to read though they are constantly surrounded by words, they can and do hear but they can't and don't listen.

Much contemporary listening centers around the television set. And by far the greater percentage of TV programming is aimed at the level of a twelve-year-old mind. How many times have you seen someone switch from one of the few good news or cultural programs—that require a little listening effort—to a program that requires no thought at all?

Unwilling to exert the energy that listening demands

But you don't have to listen all day and all night and come away with exactly the same amount of information you had before. TV offers countless opportunities today to listen to difficult though enlightening material—provided you *want* to improve your listening skills and are willing to exert the energy that trained listening demands. There are regular newscasts and special news coverage, good music and good theater, seminars and forums of all kinds, good dramatic and poetry readings—in short, a wealth of listening to practice on.

This is one listening trap we must pull ourselves out of by our own bootstraps.

Contributor No. 9 (strictly subconscious): Reacting to Loaded Words. This is the second of two contributors to bad listening which affect the emotions so that control is difficult. Every speaker runs into loaded words no matter how much he may try not to. They can crop up many many times—either in person-to-person conversation or during formal presentation. They put him at a tremendous disadvantage—in fact, loaded words can be a speaker's nemesis.

Every listener has words which disturb him

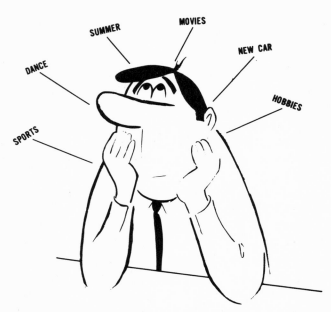

Certain words produce an instantaneous effect on bachelors, while . . .

Every listener has many words which disturb him. Most listeners know some of these words, but don't know why they are disturbing. And of course there are some words which affect people without people's being aware of them. These are the more dangerous ones. However, both types are dangerous—both to the speaker and to the listener.

When a listener discovers that a word is disturbing him every time he hears it, he should jot it down and try to learn why it affects him. This is the first big step in controlling his reaction to it. However, the speaker faces the task of learning to recognize those words which are likely to give trouble—and there are enough of them to make his job extremely difficult.

For example, certain words produce an instantaneous effect on bachelors: *sports, dance, summer, movies, hobbies, new car.* Married men, on the other hand, react strongly to

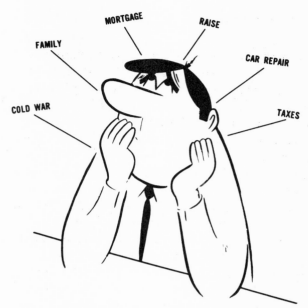

. . . married men react to words of a different sort

words of quite a different sort, such as *cold war, family, mortgage, car repair, taxes, raise.* (Perhaps bachelors, too, respond to the word *raise,* but in their case the possibilities it suggests ordinarily are far livelier.) Since most business audiences include both happy bachelors and care-worn married men, the speaker's problem is compounded over and over.

Not knowing is responsible for many of our everyday difficulties and frustrations. Simply by not knowing you subconsciously fell victim to mental dissipation and illiterate listening. Now, by just knowing these contributors to bad listening, you can make sure that they no longer work negatively against you. Instead, they should work positively—for you.

Reviewing them day by day will heighten your awareness and your listening literacy, thereby making you more valuable to your organization, your family, and yourself.

EMPATHY IN LISTENING

"Empathy" is the capacity for participating in the other person's feelings or ideas. Applied to listening, it is one of the most important ingredients in communication. But you must improve all the other elements of listening skill before you can be an "empathic" listener.

Implied here is what we term *nondirective* listening; that is, allowing the person to solve his own problems just by talking them out. The listener acts as a sounding board for the talker.

Being a sounding board isn't as easy as it sounds, however. Nondirective listening encompasses the full range of empathy; the listener must at all times remain silent, but he must clearly be interested, sincere, thoughtful, and understanding. How can you be all these and still remain silent? You merely ask no questions and show no signs of disagreement with what is being said.

There are just three responses that are allowed the listener in a nondirective listening situation. They are a nod of the head, *uh huh,* and *huh.* But be careful of the way you say *huh.* If you aren't listening carefully, it will sound as if it came from out in left field, and the speaker will know your attention was wandering.

Listening takes a great amount of energy, as we have said. It is much more difficult than talking. During your next conversation try to be consciously aware of how many times you interrupt the other party. Also, notice the frequency with which he interrupts you with no apparent thought of rudeness.

A good nondirective listener is a valuable member of the management team. More information can be gained from employees at both critical and noncritical times by this technique than by any other. But, before an employee will talk freely with management, he must have complete faith that you want to listen to him and that his confidence will not be betrayed.

This rapport is not easily established. If you ask even one question, the employee may become suspicious. He will wonder why you asked the question and what kind of answer you would really like to have. He may also think that if he gives you an honest answer he will lose prestige or monetary advantages; so he will probably give you the answer he thinks you would rather hear. Thus you have changed the whole slant of the employee's thinking and talking, and from that time on you may never get an honest answer, much less discover what the employee has to say. This in itself can be expensive.

Sometimes it takes several attempts at nondirective listening before the employee decides that he can trust you. These attempts may seem to have very little practical value, but they are more significant than you realize. It is during these initial conversations that you are being evaluated by the employee. He is then making up his mind what kind of manager you are and whether he can safely confide in you or not.

Much more difficult than talking

If he decides in the affirmative, then you immediately become more than a manager to him—you become his friend. By being his friend, you automatically become a better-informed manager, and your management responsibilities will seem lighter. Your output will increase; it will be of better quality and reliability.

Everyone enjoys working with someone he likes. He works harder and better, produces more, tries in every way to make the manager's job easier. Nobody, on the other hand, enjoys working with someone he *doesn't* like. His energy level will slump, he will produce less (and that of poor quality), and he may even try deliberately to make things harder for the boss.

You must never underestimate an individual's ability to solve his own problems just by talking them out. You must never probe for additional facts. What, then, do you do, in a nondirective listening situation, when an employee asks a question? The best approach is just to sit there contemplating it. In all probability the employee will continue talking after a few seconds. If he doesn't, you verbally ask yourself the same question.

For example, he may ask, "What would *you* do in that situation?" After thinking it over briefly, you say, "Hmm. What *would* I do?" The employee is very likely to continue his train of thought. All he wanted was to hear himself ask the question. He did not want it answered.

Most supervisors and managers have had a subordinate come up and say, "I have a problem. I hope you can help me with it." He starts describing his problem and then says suddenly, "Thanks a lot," right in the middle of a sentence. He has solved his problem just by talking it over with you. Had you shown an inclination not to listen, he might not have solved his problem at all. He would instead have been frustrated and perhaps would have developed other problems.

Failure to listen understandingly is expensive to industry. All too often an employee who wants to talk with his supervisor is put off impatiently. The supervisor either ignores him or is so disagreeable that the employee becomes upset and has to stay home for a day or more. According to Dr. Ralph T. Collins, a former president of the New York State Association for Mental Health, "Emotional illness causes more absenteeism in industry than any other illness except the common cold." [4]

What percentage of absenteeism actually is due to the lack of skilled, emphatic listening is open to question. Whatever it may be, it's too high—and it doesn't take into consideration those who are frustrated by the lack of understanding but who stay on the job at the cost of low production, dissatisfaction, and morale problems.

There are situations where the need for listening is not job-related. A domestic or personal problem may be involved. Should management take the time and spend the money to listen to it? Dr. Collins says, "Industry hires the 'whole man' and must be concerned with the entire realm of problems that affect that man on the job."

A problem is a problem; whether it is job-related or not, it affects the emotions, health, and productivity of the employee while he is on the job. There are, of course, times when professional help is needed and the manager should direct the employee to the medical department or to a doctor for further advice. If, however, empathic listening will prevent frustrations, promote good mental and physical health, reduce absenteeism, and increase production, it is worth more in morale, quality, and reliability than can be measured in dollars alone.

Nondirective listening is one of the most important of the human relations skills without which, however outstanding

[4] Talk at Harpur College, State University of New York at Binghamton, New York.

your technical or professional skills, you will never succeed for long as a manager. Develop you listening ability and you cannot help but further your management growth.

LISTENING PEAKS

The trained speaker knows that after 40 minutes most of his audience is lost—mentally. Forty minutes, that is to say, should be the maximum for the average group. Give them more than that and you're usually talking to yourself unless you're forceful and effective enough to keep people's minds from falling into those dissipation traps.

The accompanying graph shows the approximate listening span of a typical audience with its peaks and valleys. The valleys show what happens when a loaded word hits home

A TYPICAL AUDIENCE LISTENING SPAN

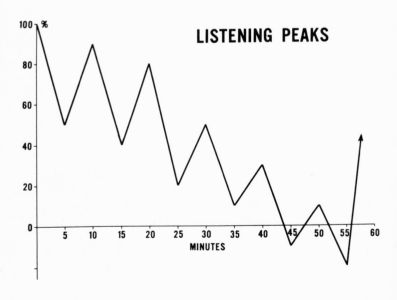

LISTENING PEAKS

—people go out on a mental tangent. Then, in a short time, they become mentally alert again and listen until another word triggers them off—and so on, over and over.

Your challenge is to keep your audience's listening peak at the top of the chart.

MEMORY AND ITS IMPROVEMENT

We use the theatrical masks of tragedy and comedy to illustrate our discussion of memory systems because tragic and comic events are generally the most memorable for us. Indeed, these two aspects of our lives—tragedy and comedy —account for approximately 50 percent of what we experience over the years. And, because this 50 percent has affected our emotions to such a degree, it can be recalled almost instantaneously. It is the other 50 percent—the gray area, the events which do not affect our emotions significantly—that we find so difficult to remember.

An electronic computer will not perform efficiently if it is not well programmed. It must have the right information correctly stored in its memory by a human being. So, too, your mental human computer—your brain—must be well programmed if it is to work efficiently. You must *consciously* make the input, *consciously* store the information

for future search and recall. Your one big problem is that you do not invariably program your mental computer properly.

As a communicator, you must keep in mind the basic systems which aid us in the input, storage, search, and recall factors of memory. Nothing is ever forgotten; it just is hard for us to recall it. That's why we spend so much time hunting through masses of paper for those missing figures.

What are these memory systems? Many of us don't know —no one has ever taught them to us. Our instructors, teachers, and professors always inundated us with information, apparently expecting us to absorb it, like sponges, and be able to give it back to them. It is, perhaps, an accomplishment of sorts to be able to hear something and then parrot it back to the speaker. However, if our teachers had taken the time to teach us the basic memory systems which we shall describe in the next few pages, more of us might have finished high school and college in six years instead of eight,

Hunting through masses of paper for those missing figures

and our professional careers could very well have advanced more rapidly.

The Whole Memory System.   In order to remember anything well, it is necessary first to understand and retain the idea or ideas underlying it. For best results, the material presented should be logically organized. The better the organization, the better the degree of retention, and this will facilitate recall. Hence the importance of listening first for the speaker's ideas, then making sure you understand those ideas, and only then substantiating those ideas with the facts.

Many people are fact grabbers. They can repeat the facts, but they cannot discuss a subject intelligently because they neither know nor understand the ideas back of the facts.

By way of contrast, let's see what a good actor does. When he first receives his script, he reads and rereads the whole thing several times. Only when he feels that he knows the plot, the interplay between the characters, and the justification for the action—all from the author's frame of reference —will he then get down to the business of learning his lines.

What has he done? He has used the whole memory system first. By discovering all that he could about the play, he has made it easier for him to learn his own part in it much more rapidly. He now understands its meaning in relationship to the script as a whole.

The same method will work for you in business as you listen to a speaker. First the ideas, then the understanding, then the facts to back up the ideas. And you can use this method in reading a report or memo—even a lengthy one. Read it all through first to discover how your knowledge or skill, your proposed contribution, or the action you are expected to take fits into the whole picture. If you do this, you won't be acquiring information that will float around somewhere in outer space.

Your children, moreover, can use the system to improve in their studies. They should first read through an assignment as a whole to get its general idea, then go back and pick out the essentials. These essentials can then be underlined for quick reference and review.

Only about 25 percent of our college students are capable of grasping the main idea of a presentation. This is the result of many factors; in general, however, students don't know where the main idea should occur. Neither do many managers. So—to go back to our precepts in Part I—if you're addressing a number of untrained listeners, for the sake of greater retention be sure you give them your material in a logical, organized sequence. Always state your main idea immediately after your opening remarks. Pause long enough between your opening remarks and your main idea so that no one will think your main idea is part of your jokes. Make sure that your transition is definite. And mention your main idea at least three times—usually at the beginning, in the middle, and at the end of your talk.

Logic, organization, and classification make up the chief props of information retention and recall. Ignore them and you haven't programmed the computer properly.

The Spaced Memory System.   You will be well on your way to improving your recall of information if you use the whole memory system faithfully. But that in itself is not enough. The spaced memory system is just as important. Its success depends on the essentials—the ideas—which can be picked out of the presentation, the preparedness of the speaker, and the utilization of the whole memory system. It is essential if storage and recall are to be effective.

Material is much easier to learn and recall if we consciously refer to it at spaced intervals—for example, several times during a day—instead of trying to absorb it all at one time. In other words, distributing learning makes forgetting slower.[5] The number of conscious referrals needed will depend on the difficulty of the material to be learned.

[5] See page 200 of Pyle's *The Psychology of Learning* (note 3).

The thought of the papers recurs

Let's say that you consciously refer to your material 30 times today, 20 times tomorrow, and 10 times the next day. If, after a significant amount of time, you refer to this material again, you are likely to retain it for only a comparatively short period of time. When, however, you are certain that you've learned the information but you want to be confident of recalling it at some later date, you bring the modified spaced memory system into use. Instead of referring to the information several times a day, you now refer to it after you retire for the evening, just prior to sleep. Then you refer to it again first thing in the morning (sometime during the middle of the day is also a good time).

Psychologists refer to this system as *overlearning*. Overlearning makes forgetting slower.[6] If practiced consciously over a period of time, it will improve your capacity for recalling specific information at any future time.

You can use the spaced memory system for a multitude of things you want to remember. Some people, for example,

[6] See page 199 of *The Psychology of Learning, op. cit.*

have difficulty in remembering items which they want to take to work. Even with the spaced memory system they may not recall these items; but the trouble is not with the system, it lies with the individual. Take the following case: After going to bed, you duly remind yourself that you must take certain papers to the office in the morning. While you're engaged in your morning ablutions, the thought of the papers recurs. You get them together and put them by the door so you won't forget them when you leave. Well, then, after you get to the office, you find that you don't have the papers. Your day is completely frustrated.

How did it happen? You didn't program your computer properly. It did just what you told it to do—it reminded you of the papers in the morning. Where you erred was in picking the papers up and putting them by the door *without giving your computer instructions to pick up the papers again before you went out the door.*

It's as simple as that. You must consciously make the right input in order to get the right output. It takes only a fraction of a second of your total conscious effort, but that precious conscious moment pays great dividends.

The Basic Laws of Association.   Although these two basic memory systems are essential to good input and recall, they can be much more effective if a third basic system is used in conjunction with them. This all-important memory system is association. All of us know that we learn any new information by associating it with whatever we already know. But in too many cases just knowing this doesn't mean that it will work effectively. Too much time is spent, unnecessarily, in learning something new; much of our so-called learning time and effort is, in fact, a complete waste. We are just spinning our wheels. Learning can take place in a much shorter period of time and with much less effort if we use the basic laws of association—consciously.

As a speaker, you should make vivid associations specifically planned for your audience. You should paint mental pictures so people can make these associations for themselves. The more associations you make, the more pictures you paint in discussing any one idea, the more information your audience will remember. This, of course, will take effort on your part, but your reward will be worth a great deal more than your effort.

Association No. 1:

Similarity

The phenomenon of identical twins

When you're involved in learning or listening (we'll say just "listening" from now on, since it's nearly impossible to listen to someone and learn nothing), associate as many of your own ideas as you can with those the speaker (or instructor) is expounding. You draw these associations, of course, from past experiences. (For example, we're all familiar with the phenomenon of identical twins.) The more similar associations you can conjure up, the easier it will be for you to recall the information you hear.

Association No. 2:

Contrast

Note physical opposites

Here again, when in a listening situation, make as many contrasting associations—that is, note as many physical opposites— as you can.

These two types of associations, similarity and contrast, are the ones most often used by the subconscious. Consequently, they are the ones that should most easily keep you in, or return you to, that desirable state of conscious awareness. Note the key word—*conscious.*

Association No. 3:

Propinquity

This is one sort of association of which, consciously, we are almost totally unaware. Yet our subconscious uses it quite often.

Basing his thinking on Aristotle's philosophical system, St. Thomas Aquinas wrote: "The Law of Propinquity implies that nearness of place, time, or some other relationship of any object

You immediately recall your uncle's trophies

in memory recalls other objects that were connected with it in a previous experience." For example, if today you witness a horrible accident at a famous historical landmark during an electrical storm, and five years from now you again visit the same historical site, you will unquestionably recall the accident in all its gory detail, particularly if another storm should arise. Or, if you're strolling through a natural history museum and come across the mounted head of a large, ferocious beast, you immediately recall your wealthy uncle's hunting trophies and the terrible toothache your aunt had the last time you were there. (You were ten, and you thought she looked exactly like one of the trophies.)

It should be obvious how often—and how effectively—this association works for you.

Association No. 4:

Whole or Part

Just as the paleontologist, confronted with a fossil bone, instantly knows the creature it came from, there are circumstances when you need to hear or see only part of certain information you possess to recall all of it vividly. Sometimes just one or two words will be enough.

To illustrate: Someone may simply mention a page in a document. You immediately recall not only the page but the name of the document, the author, the publisher, and the contents. Or someone mentions the author's first name but cannot recall his last name. You promptly supply it.

These are very simple examples; however, propinquity works with the most complex ideas. The more you use it—consciously— the more you will become acquainted with it.

The paleontologist, confronted with a fossil bone . . .

Association No. 5:

Same Species

The zookeeper and the monkey in the cage may, to the humorously critical eye, seem close relatives indeed, thus typifying another form of association. This one works very much like similarity, and you may prefer it.

Some people learn more effectively by seeing, others by listening, and still others by using the muscles. Most people, however, learn best by using a combination of all three.

So it is with the associations. Same species or similarity—it makes no difference which you use. Choose whichever you wish. Maybe you will like similarity for animate beings and same species for inanimate things.

Association No. 6:

Cause and Effect

Here we have one of the most common associations of which we are consciously aware. We all know that if we put our hand on a hot stove it will burn. We all know that the distant rumble of thunder may be the prelude to an electrical storm. We all hope that peace will follow war.

The zookeeper and the monkey in the cage may seem close relatives indeed

Cause and effect, in short, is a widely used and powerful form of association. We use it every day. Hour by hour, minute by minute, decision after decision is based on our recognition of cause and effect in business.

Association No. 7:

Matching Pairs

This, too, is an association of which we are consciously aware. If asked what goes with salt, you would no doubt say pepper. If asked what goes with bacon, you would probably say eggs. Paper—pen. Table—chair. Offending husband—irate wife. And so on.

When you listen to a presentation, you are—mainly subconsciously—matching things, animate and inanimate, on the basis of your acquired store of knowledge. Making this a conscious activity will enable you to categorize new information more efficiently.

It should be clear by now that you can use several associations for any one idea. In fact, the more logical associations you apply to anything you want to remember, the better chance you stand of recalling it almost instantly.

The distant rumble of thunder may be the prelude to an electrical storm

Offending husband—irate wife

Association No. 8:

Subject and Quality (or Object and Quality)

An association not normally used during the average presentation, this one applies to both animate and inanimate objects. It might be utilized by a personnel manager in an interviewing situation to explore the character and reliability of a prospective employee (subject and quality). You yourself might apply it to the purchase of a pen or the selection of a duck for dinner (object and quality).

We judge quality by experience . . . or by testing

Here's how it works: You buy a Brand X pen and fly 3,000 miles at 30,000 feet with it in your pocket. Upon touching down, you find ink all over your shirt; so you resolve never to buy another Brand X pen again. You discount the fact that the Brand X pen obviously wasn't designed to fly at 30,000 feet and the probable fact that any other similarly priced pen would have leaked at that altitude.

We judge quality or reliability by experience, testing, or word of mouth. Of course, the first two methods are the soundest, but many people accept quality judgments on hearsay, just as they accept rumor as gospel (and the results are about as dependable).

Quality may be good or bad, cheap or expensive, beautiful or ugly, strong or weak, soft or hard. This association is most useful in a fact-giving, fact-finding type of meeting.

Association No. 9:

Synonyms

In the illustration, you see two young men sitting at two desks. One is supposedly reading; the other is supposedly thinking. Right there, however, we must admit the possibility of a slight difference of terminology: They could be students or they

It all depends on your point of view

could be scholars. It all depends on your point of view and frame of reference.

In any case, the device of the synonym should be used more often. Once you have already made your associations, you can strengthen them by applying a synonym to whatever it is you want to be able to recall.

Association No. 10:

Sequence

Sequence as a means of association works for us relentlessly. It normally is a subconscious force but can exert a tremendous influence if we will train it to operate on a conscious level.

Nearly everything that happens does so in some sort of sequence: every year, every month, every week, every day, every minute, every second, even—more so today than ever before—every fraction of a second. The application of this natural law is manifold in business, industry, education, law—in fact, all phases of human activity.

So there you have them—ten varieties of association which can be responsible for your attaining greater heights in your chosen profession. Just reading them should start you on your

Nearly everything happens in some sort of sequence

way to greater effectiveness. Being consciously aware of them and using them constantly could mean the difference between success or failure. The choice is yours.

MORE ABOUT MEMORY SYSTEMS

Whether any one memory system is of primary or secondary importance depends on which one we need to use for results at any given time. A secondary system may be of primary importance *to you* at one time, and a primary system may be of secondary importance at another. It all depends on your needs, desires, and activity at that particular time. The important thing is that you know the systems and be able to use them for your greater effectiveness and efficiency.

Here are five memory systems that are commonly termed secondary.

The Incompleted Method. Your mind works in strange ways. Once it begins some activity, it won't let you alone until it completes that activity. You should take advantage of this aggressiveness of the mind and make it work positively for you.

For example: Whenever there's something you must do today, before you go home, and you're afraid of forgetting it, just start it—whatever it is. Your mind won't let you rest until you finish it. Even just writing a note to yourself—saying that you want to complete a certain piece of work before you leave the office—will suffice.

Try this method the next time you have such a problem (that will probably be sometime today). It will save you many an embarrassing moment.

The Motor Method. We are not the first to remark that when you can learn by seeing and hearing, you learn much better and faster. You have often heard this.

The same thing holds true with your memory. Yeu can learn by just seeing or just hearing, but you *remember* better when you both see and hear. And you can remember still more with less effort if you can get involved physically—that is, if you will let the motor system fortify the memory system.

One day a suburbanite was attempting to tighten a screw on his car door when his wife called from an upstairs window to tell him he had a long-distance telephone call. He ran into the house, took the call, and returned to the car. Still he couldn't locate the screwdriver. In desperation he looked around to see if anyone was watching. Nobody was; so he pantomimed using the screwdriver. That is, he took advantage of the motor system. Within ten seconds he had remembered where he put the screwdriver—on top of the car. Sure enough! When he reached up, there it was.

The motor memory system should be used, whenever possible, to strengthen the input and recall of memory. By connecting a muscular activity with what we are learning, we make it possible to acquire the information more rapidly and recall it more quickly. Not only does the brain *absorb* the information, but the muscles *retain* it. And the muscles never forget. It's like learning to ride a bicycle or swim: Once you teach your muscles what and how to do it, you can *always* do it.

Experiment with this system the next time you misplace something. This too will probably happen sometime today—if it hasn't already.

The Time Method. To remember, with ease, anything you want to be able to recall in either the immediate or the distant future, you must first make the corresponding mental input. It is this conscious input that makes the difference between poor and good recall.

You are your own worst enemy when it comes to recall; you expect your mind to give you the answers without any effort on your part. Take looking up a telephone number. How many times have you hunted for one and then, upon

dialing it, found it was busy and hung up? A moment later
you began to dial the number again only to discover that
you had forgotten it.

This duplication of effort and time wasting can be elim-
inated if only you will *consciously* repeat the number to
yourself and *consciously* tell your mind that you want to
remember it until someone on the other end answers the
phone. The moment of effort needed can save you time,
money, and frustrations. If your secretary doesn't already
use this system, or any of the other memory systems we
have suggested, tell her about them. You should get some
favorable feedback.

The Mental Recap Method.   There must have been a
time or two when you were shopping and suddenly dis-
covered that you didn't have all your packages. You had
lost one. When this happens, most people panic mentally;
they seldom recover their property. The next time it happens
to you, just relax and mentally review where you have been,
what stores you visited, and what you did in each one.
Chances are you'll remember just where you left your
package.

Don't retrace your steps and walk around all those stores
physically until you have first taken your mental journey.
If worse comes to worst, go to a restaurant, have something
to eat, and try your mental journey once more. Now that you
are rested, the answer is bound to come to you and you can
go straight to the right store and pick up your lost package,
umbrella, or gloves.

If you misplace something at the office—say, an important
letter or memo—just sit down and mentally recapitulate your
recent activities. Sometimes you won't be immediately successful in finding the missing item, but if you'll just relax
sufficiently to start some other activity, you'll be able to put
your finger right on it.

The Conscious Storage Method.   One of the most effective memory systems is the conscious storage method. You use it with all the other systems.

Keep in mind that we remember best those things which have a significant impact on the emotions—and that we can learn, store, and recall *anything* at some future date if we make a conscious mental note that we wish to do so. It is this brief, conscious mental activity of telling yourself that you will want to refer to particular information later on that determines whether you have a good or a bad memory. So-called bad memories are the result of failure to make the proper input.

Remember the magic words: *conscious awareness.* They will enable you to develop both your listening and your memory to a degree you never before thought possible.

REMEMBERING NAMES AND FACES

Now a word about one specific area of memory: remembering names and faces. We've left this to the last for two reasons:

1. You must be consciously aware of all we have said thus far before you can effectively improve in this area.
2. This is the one area in which most people recognize the need for improvement.

Most people fail to remember a name because they never learn it in the first place. When they meet a new associate or neighbor or friend of a friend, the introduction is handled improperly. The tendency, when introducing someone, is just to mumble the name.

Why this should be so is somewhat of a mystery. Perhaps it's because the person making the introduction doesn't recall the full name of the person he is introducing. He is, in all probability, too embarrassed to admit his lack of knowledge to the name's owner.

The following technique will keep you from being embarrassed because you can't recall a name. From this moment on, don't ever let anyone get away with a mumbled introduction. Just say to the person who is being introduced, "I'm sorry, but I didn't understand your name." This, very politely, gets the person who is doing the introducing off the hook because you direct the apology, not to him, but to the person introduced to you.

If you still don't get the name, ask for it to be repeated. If it's a new one to you, take out your little notebook and inquire how it's spelled. By now you may think that the man suspects you of being some kind of nut, but quite the contrary is true. Any intelligent person will be highly complimented to think that you are going to all this trouble to remember his name.

The next technique which you will find beneficial is to use the man's name as often as is intelligently possible during your conversation. Don't overuse it, of course, but say it often enough—consciously—to implant it in your memory. Also

You can be that much-envied person

make a mental note as to whether you want to remember the name for a short or a long period of time. But be discreet about this and make certain that you make the right decision. It could backfire on you.

You should make as many logical associations as you can while talking with a person you have just met. Example: approximate age, marriage status, number of children, ages of children, babies, hobbies, interests. Associate all these with your own situation.

Up until now, you have been using the whole memory system, getting all the information you can about the individual. At this point you should use the spaced memory system; that is, consciously refer to his name several times today, fewer times tomorrow, and still fewer times the third day. You can detach the page in your notebook on which you wrote his name and put it in front of you at your desk as a reminder.

After the third day it should be necessary to refer to the name only three times during a 24-hour period (the modified space memory system). Think of it the very last thing before you go to sleep and one of the first things that you will automatically recall the first thing in the morning will be that name. Then consciously recall it in the middle of the day.

If you will follow this procedure, you can be that much-envied person who is able to recall names and faces instantly.

MISCELLANEOUS FACTORS IN EFFECTIVE LISTENING

What else affects the attention with which your listeners will hear you out—and, of course, the degree to which they will grasp what you have to say and be able to recall it at will?

Efficiency Peaks.   One important thing to know about people you're trying to reach aurally is how wide awake and energetic they are—how efficiently they are functioning— at that particular time. Ideally they should be as full of energy as the man in our picture, but such zest and gusto can hardly be common this early in the morning. Still, it's advantageous to know just when most people's efficiency peaks are likely to occur and be guided accordingly.

The curves shown in the accompanying chart illustrate the results of surveys in which only people involved in mental situations were included. As you can see, the most productive period is approximately from 9 to 11 o'clock in the morning. The next most productive period is from approximately 2:30 to 4 P.M. Notice that the efficiency peak in the afternoon is shorter and not so pronounced as the one in the morning.

The best time, then, not only to tackle your most difficult tasks but to get the best listening results from an oral presentation is during the peak morning hours from 8:30 to 11.

Such zest and gusto can hardly be common

The afternoon hours should be saved for more routine responsibilities.

The two curves change, however, when mechanical or assembly operations are involved. The morning curve rises both much more rapidly and earlier—at approximately 8:30 —and it stays high until lunchtime. Afterward it resumes its prelunch peak almost immediately, sometimes surpassing its morning's high, and it stays up till quitting time. In the case of a secretary, interestingly enough, the curve tends to fall between these two. Why? Because at times a secretary is doing mental work; at other times, mechanical work.

These curves are based on the average person working approximately an eight-hour day. For people working the

PEAKS IN HUMAN EFFICIENCY

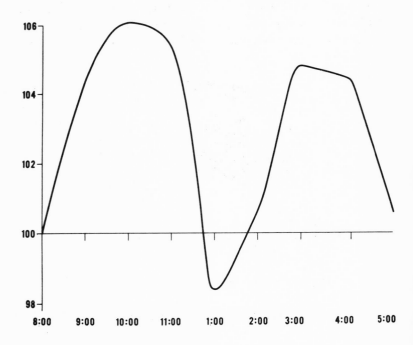

night shift, of course, the times are eight hours out of phase. And they bear no relationship whatsoever to poets, writers, actors, musicians, dancers, or anyone else in a purely creative field.

Age. Does age have anything to do with memory? That's still a debatable question. Most experts agree, however, that there's about a 5 percent factor built in; that age does affect memory to this small extent. Otherwise, if an individual is mentally and physically healthy, the only thing that will affect his memory is his own lack of desire, motivation, or will to listen, learn, retain, and recall.

It is one of any speaker's responsibilities to motivate and interest his audience, however many age levels may be represented so they will want to listen, learn, retain, and recall the information he gives them.

The only thing that will affect his memory is lack of motivation

BAIL OUT

Make sure your audience knows exactly what you mean

Semantics.   You express yourself with words, you defend and attack with words, you explain and define with words. Many times you get into a multitude of communication difficulties with words. To "bail out," for example, can mean to parachute from a plane, empty a boat of water, or procure the release of a prisoner.

Some of these communication difficulties can be prevented by ascertaining that the person or audience knows exactly what you mean by the words you use. If you must use unfamiliar terms, define them as you go along.

Much has already been written about "the semantic swamp." You will avoid it if you will try always to say exactly what you mean in the simplest possible words.

ANALYTICAL LISTENING

To be an effective communicator, there is yet another need you should be aware of. That is analytical listening.

Your listeners should anticipate your subject and mentally ask themselves what you may be intending to cover in your talk. They should mentally summarize your ideas and facts as you speak. They should weigh the speaker's evidence by questioning all facts, stories, and statistics.

- Are they accurate?
- Are they unbiased?
- Is the picture complete?

Your audience should also listen between the lines for important missing words. They should watch your facial expressions, gestures, body movements, and tone of voice.

A quick or unintentional change in a speaker's expression can tip the listener off to the fact that something is wrong, and a clumsy or a forced gesture should likewise alert the thinking listener. In the same way an abrupt change of body movement or tone of voice is a sign that the speaker is on uncertain ground. The audience should then listen and weigh critically every word he utters.

OBSERVATION WITH ALL THE SENSES

Although observation is listed second in the subtitle of this section on aural communication, we are discussing it last because we must be consciously aware of the techniques of listening and memory before the techniques of observation will be of practical value to us. It is first necessary to develop our listening and memory skills to a high degree; only then can we increase our powers of observation to that same level of effectiveness.

When we speak of observation, we don't mean seeing with the eyes alone. According to the definition which we shall use, observation is to perceive with *all the senses;* that is, to be consciously aware of using all the senses along with our knowledge of effective speaking and good listening. It is observation in this context which will have a real impact on you. Life will begin to take on new meaning and dimensions. Your relations with others will improve tremendously; you will understand people better, and you will be able to motivate and influence people as you never did before.

This greater insight into what makes people behave as they do results from the fact that, by this time, you are beginning to understand yourself better. You realize that people see you, not as you see yourself, but for what they see in you. You realize that you have not really known yourself very well—so how can other people know you?

By sharpening your senses you sharpen your interpersonal skills. You become much more sensitive to everyone around you. In short, you develop your *sense-itivity* toward your fellow man to a degree which may just be to your future success as a manager, as a husband and father, and simply as a friend.

Remember your many challenges as a communicator. Remember that you are only 50 percent prepared when you are 100 percent prepared in oral communication. You are 100 percent prepared as a communicator when you are both orally prepared as a speaker and consciously aware of the aural unpreparedness—the illiterate listening habits—of your audience and you have the knowledge and ability to deal with them.

Learn how to observe that audience, the recipients of your message, with all your senses and there should be no question of your communication skill—whether on the speaker's platform, in a conference or committee meeting, or in day-to-day conversation.

III. CONFERENCE LEADERSHIP
Communication Skills Applied

The Conference Memo. Leader and Participant. Some Untoward Situations: The Uncontrolled Conference, The Star Performer, The Uninvited Guest, Those Inevitable Distractions, The Late Arrival, The Urgent Message. Simple Methods of Control: Order Out of Chaos, The Tactful Squelch, First Aid for the Introvert. The Problem Solved.

The drawings in Part III are the work of Douglas Chaffee.

This handbook on oral and aural communication would be incomplete if it did not contain a short section on how the suggested methods and techniques can be of practical value in the problem-solving conference. Section III, then, should aid you in applying the lessons learned in Sections I and II; for clearly, to be successful either as a conference leader or as a conference participant in modern business and industry, it is necessary to be a sensitive listener as well as an effective speaker.

Right now, let's define just what a conference is intended to do. We shall limit ourselves here to the *problem-solving* conference. Therefore, the following definition should suffice: The purpose of a conference is to arrive at a logical and practical solution to a problem in the shortest possible period of time.

This purpose is accomplished by working with and through the participants. A conference is a constructive situation that encompasses a team effort. It is a talking-together and working-together effort. It calls for the kind of dedication which terminates in a creative approach to problem solving.

Much unnecessary time is lost in conferences solely because the leader does not keep the discussion firmly centered on the immediate subject in hand.

THE CONFERENCE MEMO

The first, and one of the most important, requirements for a successful conference, is the memo. It must be designed to give the prospective attendees all the information they should know concerning the conference. It should also be designed to transmit this information in the smallest possible space.

Today's executives just don't have the time to peruse a lengthy memo to locate the information they need. To bury this information in the body of a memo is doing just that—wasting time.

The memo should be short and to the point. One sentence or, at most, a brief paragraph is enough to explain the purpose of the conference (or the agenda). The date, time, and place should be pulled out of the body and set down separately. Another short sentence to request that all attendees please be on time, a similarly brief notation as to the approximate length of the conference, plus a list of the attendees—there you have all you need in a good strong action memo. On page 103 is an ideal standard which demands action and requires a minimum of time to read.

LEADER AND PARTICIPANT

It is, of course, of prime importance that each conference participant be both heard and understood if everyone is to listen intelligently. Conversely, it is also necessary that the participants *listen* intelligently so they can *respond* intelligently.

The Conference Leader.   A skillful conference leader can control, guide, develop, and get quick results in a comparatively short period of time. Fair to all, he not only gets

February 8, 19—

TO:

J. R. Narns	J. H. Boberts
J. C. Donnelly	P. J. Tiltsey
R. E. Doty	E. F. Laterico
E. N. Linjop	O. L. Kaulker
G. E. Nady	R. N. Scold
A. J. Lokanda	J. P. Miomek

SUBJECT:

You are requested to attend a conference to discuss the feasibility of three equal shifts.

TIME:	9:14 A.M. to 12:45 P.M.
DATE:	Monday, February 27, 19—.
PLACE:	Room 3.
BLDG:	300-3.

Please be on time.

John P. Grimes
Dept. 000
Extension 8888

JPG:fgq

He gets respect—but not with a gun in either hand

the respect of the attendees but keeps it—and not with a gun in either hand à la TV Westerns.

The best conference leader has had ample training in the principles and techniques of communication, both oral and aural. Applying them to the problem-solving conference has become second nature to him. Whatever the situation, he is seldom at a loss—and never for long.

The conference leader remembers at all times, simply because he is the leader, that he doesn't want to embarrass or insult anyone. This group for which he is responsible has been called together because the individual members, each contributing his know-how and working amicably with the others, can help solve a specific problem. It is the leader's job to make this happen.

The Conference Participant. The best conference participant, like the best conference leader, has had training in both speaking and listening.

The next time you attend a conference, just sit there and listen to every participant who has something to say. Take notes about points on which you agree and disagree. Then, after everyone in the room has expressed himself pro or con, you will have more information at your fingertips than all the rest of the group put together.

Now is the moment for you to take the floor. Everyone else has spoken his piece, and so you, armed with all your notes, have the best opportunity to set forth your views. It's like having the rail position in a race—the correct timing and placement can mean the difference between losing or winning.

A well-informed person is not only an excellent conversationalist but an efficient and effective conference participant. And, remember, many promotions have been granted—and will again be granted—because someone knew how to be a good conference leader or a good conference participant—or both.

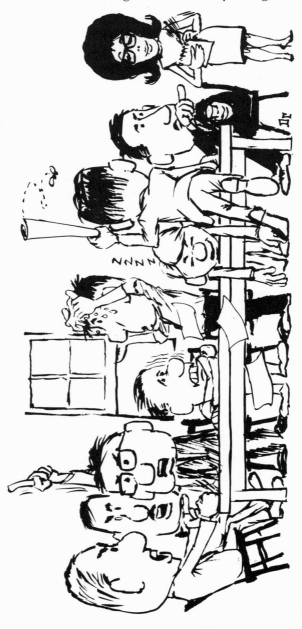

Some conferences end up in sheer chaos

SOME UNTOWARD SITUATIONS

What are some common conference difficulties? Let's cite a few along with some do's and don'ts for handling them.

The Uncontrolled Conference.   No doubt you've attended conferences which ended up in sheer chaos. You came away with absolutely nothing to show for your time.

Whoever the conference leader may be in our illustration, he obviously has no effective control over the group. Everyone is talking at the same time, and nothing is being accomplished. This is one reason why so many executives dislike attending conferences. What is needed is a forceful conference leader who can take control at the start and not lose it.

The Star Performer.   Many conferences fail because they have one or more star performers. Actually there's no place for a star performer in *any* conference. This type of person dominates, or tries to dominate, the whole session. He constantly interrupts, ridicules comments from others, and is a general nuisance throughout the meeting.

It's unfortunate enough when an attendee tries to play the role of star performer, but when the conference leader assumes that role, the meeting usually turns out to be just a vehicle for him. A conference should be dominated by no one. The leader should encourage all the members to participate and not attempt to run the show by himself.

To be successful, a conference must elicit cooperation and teamwork. Everyone must contribute. If one man has all the answers, the conference isn't needed.

The Uninvited Guest.   It is unnerving to discover, suddenly, that there is an uninvited guest at your conference. Yet an amazing number of people attend meetings uninvited —it seems as though they have nothing else to do. In fact, one self-invited guest whose name wasn't on the memo nonchalantly informed the chairman that he didn't have any-

The star performer dominates, or tries to dominate, the whole session

thing pressing at the moment so he thought he would drop in to see what was going on.

If you happen to be a conference leader and an uninvited guest turns up, it's your responsibility to request him, as politely as you can, to leave. Of course, if the vice president of the company drops in, you give him exactly the same treatment you always give the president—invited or uninvited!

Those Inevitable Distractions. It goes without saying that the conference room must be chosen with care. It should be an inside room, with few potential distractions and the thermostat at a comfortable setting. Outside rooms usually are hot at one end and cold at the other, if only because people are busy fighting the battle of the windows.

There are the well-known clock watchers, fly swatters, and secretary watchers, all of whom are difficult to control, but a wise choice of conference room should eliminate most of them. This, too, is one of the responsibilities of the conference leader.

The Late Arrival. Not only does everybody in the room turn toward the person who arrives late, but he usually stumbles over several people before he gets to his appointed place. This is not only inconvenient for the rest of the group but also discourteous. If you have an empty chair, be sure it's near the entrance door so the late arrival can sit without needlessly disrupting the conference.

The Urgent Message. A message runner is still another disrupter of conferences. Try to keep messages to a minimum to avoid having to stop the meeting while they're first signed for, then read, then dealt with as necessary.

SIMPLE METHODS OF CONTROL

If a conference involves ten people, and the average number of years' experience represented by each participant

The secretary watcher is difficult to control

is ten, there are 100 years of experience from which to draw. It would seem highly improbable that any group of problem solvers with 100 years of experience at their disposal could be doomed to failure, yet conferences with as much as 200, 300, and 400 years often fail because (1) the leader fails to conduct the session properly and (2) the other members fail to participate constructively.

Order Out of Chaos.   Most conferences get out of hand if emotions are stirred. This can easily happen when controversial matters are being discussed: reorganization, shifting job responsibilities, human relations, personnel problems, second- and third-shift operations, cafeteria schedules—especially parking space.

Private side conferences can occur even while a participant has the floor. Many conference leaders just let the situation continue until the speaker has finished—or is finished. This, of course, shows a lack of leadership control—the leader should never force a speaker to continue while private conversations are going on.

What to do? The obvious first step is just to ask the speaker to wait until quiet has been restored. In itself, this is usually enough to make the wrongdoers aware that they are disrupting the conference. You've mentioned no names and accused no one; consequently no feelings are hurt and no animosities have been created. The conversationalists probably feel sheepish or guilty. They apologize, and the meeting continues.

But there are times when it isn't as simple as that. Once in a while a side conversation will continue even after your mild reprimand. If it does exceed what you consider to be an unreasonable time, then you as leader must request that the conference come to order. Even now you're mentioning no names, so that no feathers are ruffled.

There are, of course, individuals with whom neither silence nor a verbal request is effective. It then becomes necessary to do one (or both) of two things:

Private side conferences can occur even while a participant has the floor

1. Ask the conversationalists if they would care to share their information with the rest of the group. Sometimes this works very positively; the offenders say, "Yes, we would." So you thank them but ask if they could possibly hold it until the present speaker has finished.
2. If this fails, call the offending participants by name, tell them they're disrupting the conference, and suggest that if their information is pertinent to the topic under discussion, everyone would appreciate having it—later. This usually does it, but the full treatment must be used only as a last resort—and never in angry tones. Normally the guilty parties aren't aware that they are breaking all the rules of the game.

The Tactful Squelch.   You will, of course, avoid monopolizing the proceedings yourself, but how about the occasional participant who does his best to take over? There is, for instance, the extreme extrovert who will never, willingly, relinquish the floor. He's not *intentionally* the star-performer type; his performance is just part of his personality. Still, he must be controlled.

The most effective method of handling him is to place him on your extreme right or left. There he can keep raising his hand for attention while you look straight ahead or, better yet, away from him. If he does accidentally catch your eye, you can put him off for a time with whispers.

Why invite him in the first place? Supposedly, because he can contribute to the conference. So, although at times he's obstreperous, you tolerate him. But you can and do control him.

First Aid for the Introvert.   The other type of conference participant that must be considered when arranging your seating plan is the introvert. To place him in the center or at the extreme end of the table is disastrous. He has information to offer, but he just cannot bring himself to express himself in a group, especially when there is even one extro-

Place him on your extreme right or left

verted star performer ready and willing to take charge. The extrovert, often quite unconsciously, overwhelms the introvert, who just clams up.

The correct place for this fellow is beside you. When you get to that point in the conference where you know he can contribute, you address him directly. Then, typically, he looks at *you*, talks to *you* in a quiet voice, rather as if there were no one else present. You repeat what he's said to the rest of the group, and the conference continues from there. Each time information is needed from him, the same procedure is followed.

THE PROBLEM SOLVED

To repeat our definition: The purpose of a conference is to arrive at a logical and practical solution to a problem in the shortest possible period of time. To this end, the specific purpose of the specific conference is stated in the memo of invitation. It should also be written on the blackboard before the conference begins.

You probably can recall conferences where what you thought was the problem in question wasn't the problem at all. That isn't at all unusual. Sometimes the sole function of a conference is to determine the problem. Only then can you proceed to solve it. Sometimes, too, the revealing discovery is made that the major problem is just an accumulation of minor problems which were not taken care of at the right time. Once these minor problems are disposed of, the major problem disappears.

There is no need to go into the details of drawing up a conference agenda and using it as a guide to conducting the meeting. Probably you already know these details; if you don't, you can get them in a good text on conference leadership. What is helpful, however, is a concise outline of proce-

The introvert just cannot bring himself to speak up in a group

ОтальнооффOFF

CONFERENCE LEADERSHIP PROCEDURES

[Developed by Ward Van Orman, IBM Space Guidance Center, Huntsville, Alabama]

I. Preparation (before conference)

   A. Select participants.
   B. Reserve room.
   C. Collect data and audio-visual aids.
   D. Appoint leader and recorder.
      Write memo to participants listing:
      tentative agenda, time, date, and place.

II. Approach to Decision (during conference)

   A. Define *real* problem(s) and motivate group.
     1. Discuss tentative agenda.
     2. List apparent problem(s); then
     3. Select FINAL AGENDA OF REAL PROBLEMS.
   B. List all possible solutions to problems.
   C. Eliminate, rearrange, and combine possible solutions.
   D. Select best possible solutions/combinations.
   E. Assign responsibilities for action:
     1. Most assignments should be voluntary.
     2. No assignments should be assumed by the leader. He should leave himself free for advice and assistance.

III. Follow-up (after conference)

   A. Recorder: Distribute minutes to participants.
   B. Participants: Fulfill assignments; keep leader posted.
   C. Leader: Assist participants with individual assignments and reports.
   D. Leader: Plan follow-up conferences when necessary (repeating above procedures).

The conference leader must motivate the group to want *success*

dures for the leader to follow before, during, and after the conference. The one on page 117 has been used successfully for many years.

But the most logically outlined leadership procedures are not enough; *motivation* plays a significant part in the success or failure of any conference. Just the fact that the attendees were invited because they were knowledgeable about the subject to be discussed is no guarantee.that the meeting will be productive. The conference leader must motivate the group to *want* success.

You must therefore find a common link or goal between the purpose of the conference and the participants and endeavor to relate the purpose to the participants. You must make everyone feel that he has a specific part to play in the proceedings and that the results will reflect—favorably or unfavorably—upon him.

These, in summary, are the significant essentials for a successful problem-solving conference. Today's business, industry, and education need highly trained people to make the most of this management tool. You, the manager or professional man, can excel as a conference leader and participant if you will focus on developing your oral and aural communication skills. Improve these and you will improve your chances of advancement.

A Final Word

To be absolutely certain that your recipient receives all your message, you must articulate, enunciate, pronounce, and project your words properly. Your hands must be nowhere near your mouth or face when you are speaking. Many messages—some of them important—are completely lost just because of this one bad habit of letting your hands interfere with your speech.

Here are a few general tips for better communication, not only in business and professional life but in all person-to-person situations:

- Use short descriptive sentences when giving a message.
- Delete any extraneous material.
- Emphasize the important words in your message.
- Use simple, not complex words, for accuracy.
- Use correct but not stilted grammar.
- Mentally organize your thoughts in a logical sequence before transmitting your message.
- Make your message as brief as possible.

By all means be courteous whenever communicating a message or instructions. Usually, most of what you say will be lost or misinterpreted if the recipient's emotions become more than normally involved. Of course, there are occasions when your plan is definitely to stimulate the emotions of your recipient.

Strive for empathy. Put yourself in the recipient's place. Try to understand his point of view.

Be absolutely certain that in your communication you answer the six questions *what, where, when, why, how,* and *who.* (The answer to the *why* will of course change at different levels of management and nonmanagement.) Any message will be more accurately relayed if the person for whom it is intended has the answer to these questions and is left in no doubt as to what you expect him to do.

The importance of increasing your message's chances of being received successfully is obvious: Messages must be acted upon as well as understood. In short—and this is one of the messages of this book—the sender is every bit as responsible for the accuracy of communicated information as the person or persons at whom it is directed.

Oral and aural communication, in a nutshell, is a 50:50 proposition.

Other Books You May Want to Read

Atkinson, William Walker, *The Art of Logical Thinking*, The Progress Company, Chicago, 1909.

Bernstein, Theodore M., *Watch Your Language*, Channel Press, Manhasset, N.Y., 1958.

Bobbitt, Joseph M., "Help Your Brain Work for You," *Nation's Business*, April 1958, pp. 86–88.

Brown, Milton, *Effective Supervision*, The Macmillan Company, New York, 1956.

Chase, Stuart, *Guide to Straight Thinking*, Harper & Brothers, New York, 1956.

Church, C. A., "You Can Communicate More Skillfully," *General Electric Review*, Vol. 60 (1957), pp. 35–37.

Drucker, Peter F., *The Effective Executive*, Harper and Row, New York, 1967.

Garrett, Eileen, *Awareness*, Garrett Publications, New York, 1943.

Hayakawa, S. I., *Language in Action*, Harcourt, Brace & Company, New York, 1940.

Irving, Paul H., "Studies in Remembering," in George S. Klein (ed.), *Psychological Issues*, Vol. 1, International Universities Press, Inc., New York, 1959.

Koehler, Alan, *The Madison Avenue Speech Book*, McGraw-Hill Book Company, New York, 1964

Lee, Irving J., *How To Talk With People*, Harper & Brothers, New York, 1952.

Monroe, Alan H., *Principles and Types of Speech,* Scott, Fores-
man & Company, Chicago, 1962.

Moore, John, *You English Words,* J. B. Lippincott Company,
Philadelphia, 1961.

Nichols, Ralph G., "Listening Is Good Business," *Management of
Personnel Quarterly,* Winter 1962, pp. 2–10.

————, and Leonard A. Stephens, *Are You Listening?* McGraw-
Hill Book Company, New York, 1957.

Parker, Willard E., and Robert W. Kleemeier, *Human Relations
in Supervision,* McGraw-Hill Book Company, New York, 1951.

Reilly, William J., *The Twelve Rules for Straight Thinking,* Harper & Brothers, New York, 1947.

Rugg, Harold, *Imagination,* Harper & Row, New York, 1963.

Stewart, Nathaniel, "Listen to the Right People," *Nation's Business,* January 1963, pp. 60–63.

Stone, W. Clement, and Norma Lee Browning, *The Other Side
of the Mind,* Prentice-Hall, Inc., Englewood Cliffs, N.J., 1964.

Techniques of Conference Leadership, Conference Board Reports, Studies in Personnel Policy No. 77, National Industrial
Conference Board, New York, 1955.

Wood, Frederick T., *Training in Thought and Expression,* Macmillan & Company Limited, London, 1953.

Zelko, Harold P., *Successful Conference and Discussion Techniques,* McGraw-Hill Book Company, New York, 1957.

About the Author

J. CAMPBELL CONNELLY teaches "Listening, Observing, and Remembering"—a course he himself created and developed—to all levels of management and nonmanagement personnel at the IBM Federal Systems Division, Electronics Systems Center, Owego, New York. He holds seminars for marketing personnel and select management groups, and he conducts management development sessions.

Mr. Connelly attended the Pace Institute of Business and is a graduate of the National Academy of Theatre Arts. For more than 15 years, he has made a specialty of courses and workshops in speech, personal development, and creative development for both industrial and educational organizations. He also organized and directed the only creative dramatics, children's theater, and adult theater in industry in the United States. He frequently addresses educational, managerial, military, business, civic, and cultural groups.